APPARENTLY I KNOW WHO SATAN IS

Apparently I Know Who Satan Is

My Fight Against Maturity and Other Irritating Social Norms

Thanks very much for your support Cross!

SARA J. FORD

SEABOARD PRESS

JAMES A. ROCK & COMPANY, PUBLISHERS

Apparently I Know Who Satan Is:
My Fight Against Maturity and Other Irritating Social Norms by Sara J.Ford

SEABOARD PRESS

is an imprint of JAMES A. ROCK & CO., PUBLISHERS

Apparently I Know Who Satan Is: My Fight Against Maturity
and Other Irritating Social Norms copyright ©2009 by Sara J. Ford

Special contents of this edition copyright ©2009 by Seaboard Press

Address comments and inquiries to:
SEABOARD PRESS
900 South Irby Street, #508
Florence, South Carolin 29501
E-Mail:
jrock@rockpublishing.com   lrock@rockpublishing.com
Internet URL: www.rockpublishing.com

Trade Paperback ISBN-13/EAN: 978-1-59663-628-6

Library of Congress Control Number: 2008920043

Printed in the United States of America

First Edition: 2009

To Kim

for figuring out
how to get latex out of
my eyebrows without
having to shave them off
and for promising to stick around
to play that delicate role
again and again

Contents

A Schitzu Disclaimer
and a Bit About the Book

This is a coming of age tale of sorts, despite the fact that the remarkably idiotic behavior discussed in early chapters is no less present in later chapters, after which age has, as they say, come. These stories are true as far as my memory will allow them to be so, though conveniently, now that my hips will no longer accommodate one, my mother insists she never had anything against the Big Wheel. The names of two Shitzus and a few other characters have been changed in the name of common decency.

Unlike the bulk of contemporary women's coming of age tales, these are not stories about getting or keeping or attracting or losing or manipulating men. These perennial themes have been left out for two reasons: I'm a lesbian who's never taken much time to worry about such things, and I find, in general, that women straight and gay tend to lead daily lives that are far more interesting than such stories would suggest. The Great Dame Dignity doesn't wait for prom nights, first dates, or weddings to threaten abandonment, though I don't doubt her fickle nature creates problems at such times. Turns out, she can flee the premises at any moment.

Part 1

Life as a Lightning Bolt Motorcycle Stunt Person

When I was a little girl, I was driven by two primary ambitions. One was to be constantly moving, and the other was to eat candy nonstop, preferably while in motion. To point out possible correlations between these two behaviors is pointless because I won't listen. In my adult life, when people tell me that anxiety is linked to sugar intake and that maybe I could pay attention to the number of sugar-coated jellied orange slices I eat, my eyes glaze over and I wait for their lips to stop moving. Anyway, pursuant to my girlhood ambitions, my goal as a five-year-old was to get a motorcycle until I was old enough to become a professional athlete or acrobat and to eat a whole lot of Jujubes, Peeps, and Good-n-Plentys along the way.

But in the early seventies, little girls in the Midwest were not often given their own motorcycles, and I was, as we all must be, a product of my short-sighted generation. So, more appropriately, I tried to live out my fantasies through toys, though procuring just the right toys in my family was often every bit as difficult as procuring motorcycles.

In 1969, Neil Armstrong and Buzz Aldrin walked on the moon. And they were of the impression, as we are often reminded, that their stroll up there represented one giant leap for mankind.

3

Well that's a pretty dramatic phrase. Sure, the moon is impressively far away and getting up there is no doubt complicated, but thirty-seven years later, the rest of us mankind members are still waiting for our turn on the moon's surface. And we're not exactly on the verge of interplanetary bar-hopping or multi-orbital cultural awareness programs. So I don't know if the phrase fits, exactly.

More important for many of us that year was the giant leap reflected by an invention unveiled right here on mother earth. Better than an inspirational television moment prompting people to wax mystically about the forms of space travel that might *someday* be possible, this was a leap that had immediate implications. This technological advance brought autonomy to millions of people previously denied it. It changed the way individuals thought about speed and mobility and style not because it allowed them to dream about someday having speed and mobility and style but because it gave them all that and more. The real giant leap for mankind made in 1969 occurred four months prior to Apollo's lunar landing. It was the introduction, during New York's toy fair, of the magnificent, red, blue, and yellow Big Wheel.

I was only two at the time, and living in Nebraska, but even at that young age and remote location I must have known on an intuitive, toddler level that some cosmic shift had taken place. Over the next few years, as it began to make appearances on neighborhood driveways and sidewalks, I recognized at once the brilliant design of the Big Wheel. It was a beautiful machine. Its center of gravity was low, just inches off the ground, which meant one could whip this way and that at whatever speed without much risk of death. It had an adjustable seat, allowing its proud rider the perfect reach to its blue pedals, and it had plastic tassels hanging off of its super cool, wide handle bars.

Most important was the shape of the thing. The way you sat in a Big Wheel allowed you to crank on those pedals with every muscle in your body, forcing the massive front wheel to propel you down the sidewalk at previously unheard of speeds. And you had to lie back just so to get it right. Sit up too much and you didn't have the muscle to go fast. Sit back too far and your weight was over the rear wheels, which meant the front wheel lacked the necessary pressure to grip the sidewalk. Once you learned to settle your weight on your butt, though, and to spread pressure evenly between the backrest and the pedals, you understood, sitting so very close to the ground, precisely what it meant to fly.

I never got a Big Wheel though, and I'm still pissed about that. Somehow—I remain a bit murky on the exact connections here—the slayings of Kennedy and King and the Vietnam War and Richard Nixon and Pete Seeger convinced my parents that obnoxiously big, brightly colored plastic toys led to the wrong kind of childhood.

Our home décor was based on macramé and corduroy earth tones, and a Big Wheel would have seemed as out of place in our home as did the red and purple Now-n-Later wrappers stuffed under my pillowcase and falling out of my pockets. Big Wheel families were different somehow. They were less likely to have parents who'd marched on Washington and who, in 1974, started substituting tofu in traditional chicken dishes as if no one would notice. I didn't fail to get a Big Wheel because I was a girl, though I would have been the first girl on our block to own one, but rather because my parents considered us somehow above Big Wheels. As if there is such a place.

In the neighborhood, I was reduced to the status of a beggar. I was constantly asking the neighborhood boys for a chance to practice the spin-outs the toys were most famous for, and I'd hang around until the races were over and nearly everyone had gone home waiting for the opportunity. Or, if negotiating with a child fortunate enough to own multiple generations of Big Wheels, I'd be given the one out back, the one so torn up that its front wheel had gashes in it longer than a cat. The magnificent design of the toy meant that even in this deteriorated state the Big Wheel still moved, though it did so with the grace and speed my own body was used to and therefore offered little in the way of enhanced mobility.

However, despite my parents' objection to the brightly-colored plastic toys I preferred and a very different set of obstacles involving some other relatives and their bizarre gift-giving practices, I did, eventually, become the proud owner of a toy every bit as cool as the Big Wheel. This is not to say that I've ever discarded my passion for the Big Wheel. I'd buy one this afternoon if they sold them in my size, and I'd ride it to the coffee shop around the corner every morning and to the drug store for candy every afternoon.

Anyway, every November, my grandmother would call from California and ask my brother and me to produce Christmas wish lists. I appreciated the gesture, as gifts from far-away relatives who asked were far more likely to be good ones than gifts form far-away relatives who didn't ask. At least I could point the gift givers in the direction of toys as a category and away from the clothes, school supplies, and big-headed ceramic knick knacks for which I had no use.

Every year my brother and I approached our list-making duties with great care, making sure that the requests were as detailed as possible so as to minimize the potential for error. Often, my brother would get precisely what he asked for: a new wrench set, *The Physical Laws of Nature*, 3rd Edition, or a subscription to *Boys' Life Magazine*. But most years I'd get something that held no relation whatsoever to the items on my list, and my mom would get a phone call from my grandparents, during which they'd apologize and explain that in California stores, they didn't sell Nerf footballs or archery sets for girls and that they hoped I'd enjoy my new spinning-ballerina jewelry box instead.

In November of 1974, I sat my seven-year-old self down with pencil and paper, and, boldly putting all of my eggs in one proverbial basket, wrote a single-item list to help my grandparents with their holiday shopping. Before mailing it, I showed the letter to my parents, so that they too could see the depth of my yearning. This way, I figured, I doubled my still razor-thin chances.

In simple, three-to-four word sentences, I identified, described, and drew a picture of the toy I thought I'd die without, the Evel Knieval stunt man, which came with a motorcycle and launching platform. The motorcycle was heavy and it had rubber tires that gripped the floor. Its weight made it feel like a real motorcycle, if a tiny one, and the launching ramp made it race down the sidewalk with impressive authority. It could go twenty yards or more if you knew what you were doing, and it was so sturdy that it could plow into curbs without sustaining serious damage. It came with stunt ramps, so Evel could jump through a cardboard ring printed with flames or over family pets, beds of tulips, and dolls borrowed from a neighbor's living room while she was napping.

Well I didn't get Evel Knieval for Christmas, of course, because my parents thought it hideous and my grandparents thought it inappropriate. But my grandparents did come through for me that year. To my great surprise, the stores in California *did* sell an Evel Knieval doll for girls. Her name was Derry Daring, and, like Evel, she came with a serious, heavy motorcycle and a launching ramp. Like Evel, she wore a stunt suit, and both her helmet and her bike were adorned with beautiful racing stripes.

I didn't care a bit that she had breasts that protruded from her too-tight jacket, or that her eyes were eight times larger than they should have been and coated in painted-on make-up. And pink wasn't the color I would have chosen for her outfit or bike decals, but at least it was bright and flashy and in no way related to earth tones. And what's more, she had a sparkly silver swoosh running all the way down the center of her body suit, making her seem a bolt of lightning in a hot pink sky. She was my first and only action doll, and she was splendid. The fact that my gender-specifically-inclined grandparents bought such a thing for me seemed nothing short of a miracle. I loved it.

Playing with Derry Daring meant moving beyond my usual

limitations. If my own body wasn't up to the task at hand, Derry's always was, and I got to experience the thrills of flight, high speed, and general recklessness this way. I recognized her potential to live out my dreams as a lightning bolt motorcycle stunt person on a sugar high and we two commenced to behave accordingly.

Over and over again, Derry performed jumps and raced down sidewalks and driveways and hallways. When her motorcycle lost its oomph, it slowed down until it fell over and skidded to a stop. Since this was an unacceptable way for my fantasy alter-ego's motorcycle stunt rides to end, I'd run to catch up with her and quickly scoop her up, so that I could hold her upright and bring her to the real end of her run with a flashy, slow-motion spin-out, the sort I'd never had the chance to perfect on a Big Wheel.

Derry rode her motorcycle out of most of our second story windows, usually waving with one hand to the admiring and imaginative crowds before falling on gardens and driveways and ripping her useless homemade paper-napkin parachute on bushes. Derry and I loved to climb trees so that we could spy on my brother and other assorted creatures. I could climb trees without Derry, but having her with me opened up all sorts of new possibilities. Regular Joe squirrel, three years of age, would be sitting on a lower tree branch, arrogantly chirping at a cat on the lawn below, and out of nowhere a pink, booby, action hero with long blond hair and huge blue eyes would come flying through the sky toward him, threatening Joe's very existence and scaring him so badly he'd fall out of the tree.

In the small but intimidating patch of woods behind our house, Derry gave me courage to explore the places only older kids frequented. I learned to hurl her ahead of me into unknown territory, knowing I'd have to follow to retrieve her. In this way, Derry and I discovered the plastic bags and paint cans left behind by paint-sniffing teenagers. She showed me snake skins and brandy bottles and random abandoned car parts, and her sparkling, synthetic stunt suit never seemed worse for the wear.

And Derry did teach me about courage, so much so that eventually I started stepping in when her body wasn't able to perform a certain task. When I was eleven, my family moved into a big old house, and my bedroom was on the third floor. The window in my room offered a fine view of the front lawn, and about seven feet below it was a giant green-and-white striped awning providing shade and tacky decoration for the window below mine. Since I was used to hurling Derry out of second story windows at the old house, I quickly began experimenting with motorcycle jumps and free falls at this new height, paying the same amount of attention to the awning below as any other eleven-year-old lightning bolt motorcycle stunt person would.

But soon after we moved in, that awning caused some significant trouble. My friend Lisa was over to play one afternoon, and we did our usual best to irritate my brother by sorting through his things in his absence. In the attic my brother kept a new and beloved billiard-like game that I was not supposed to play with unless I had his permission, which of course I never did unless I asked for it nicely which of course was out of the question.

The game included green and red wooden discs which had holes in their middles, and it just so happened that those holes fit perfectly around Derry's arms. Derry could ride her motorcycle with no hands because her legs were strong enough to grip the motorcycle alone. And so the wooden discs gave me the idea of a new stunt Derry could perform. She'd fly through the air tumbling thirty feet to the ground on her motorcycle, and she'd do it all wearing impressively heavy, green and red weights on her upraised arms, thrilling the imaginary audience members who had heretofore thought Evel Knievel's leap over fifty cars in Los Angeles was something.

So out the window Derry flew with four discs on each upraised arm, and Lisa and I delighted in watching as the bike, helmet, seven wooden discs, and Derry herself landed all over our front lawn and in our bushes. But there was a snag. The eighth disc fell into the awning and stayed there nestled in the folds of the heavy green fabric.

I crept downstairs covertly to retrieve the other discs from the lawn, and then I put Ben's game back together like it had been, all set up for a new match, but there was no hiding the missing piece. He'd be furious. So I looked to Derry for courage and ideas. Lisa and I used electrical tape to attach Derry to the end of a cue stick and then lowered her down carefully out the window, hanging by our waists and reaching down as far as we could. We flicked at and brushed the game piece, but Derry's stiff body was not substantial enough to knock it off the awning, and I finally agreed that it was no use.

That's when I had my epiphany. It occurred to me that I didn't need to keep relying on Derry when things got rough. As we'd established time and again back in the woods, I was brave too. And what's more, I could kick the wooden disc with my own foot, or even grip it with my hand if I needed to. Maybe it was just a matter of lowering *me* out the window. Perhaps, I thought, this was what Derry had been trying to tell me all along. Her encouraging voice whispered to me like she was my very own personal Yoda, "*You already are a lightning bolt motorcycle stunt person ... You know what to do, and now you must act.*"

In my memory the theme song to *Chariots of Fire* started playing then, even though the movie didn't actually come out for four more years. We gathered a thick rope that had been used for a tire swing at the old house from our basement, and tied it roughly around my waist, then to Lisa's waist, and then to a doorknob and a stairway railing. We were serious about safety, after all.

Feet first and holding onto the rope, I made my way out the window. The house was stucco with strips of wood here and there for decoration, and since the strips of wood stuck out a half inch or so, I could use them for toe and hand rests. I lowered myself toward the awning while Lisa held onto the rope inside my room.

The wind outside startled me at first, and I looked out across the street and down the block, aware that my body was somewhere it maybe shouldn't be—twenty five feet up in the air, to be precise. But I reasoned that in my new role as an actual lightning bolt motorcycle stunt person, I'd have to do a lot of risky things, and this gave me all the courage I needed. I refocused, found a new toe hold, and continued to scale down the front of the house. Soon I was close enough to touch the awning with my foot. I stretched out my leg toward the game piece, and I kicked it off the awning, hearing it land in the bushes below.

The climb up wasn't too hard, I suppose because I was lucky and filled with adrenaline. And I collapsed onto the floor of my room a success at the very same moment that Lisa's dad pulled his car to the front curb and started walking toward our house, no more aware of what we'd just done than my own parents sitting downstairs in the kitchen had been. I don't know why none of the neighbors called to report that an eleven-year-old girl was scaling the outside of the house. I suppose they thought that's just the way young kids are these days.

From my position on the floor, I noticed that I was lying very close to Derry, and as we looked at one another—she crudely taped to the discarded cue stick, me crudely tied to a rope—I understood that I would soon move on in life without my trusted pink friend. I didn't need a lightning bolt motorcycle stunt doll if I could do things better than a lightning bolt motorcycle stunt doll, and so I took her off of the cue stick and stuck her on my dresser, heading downstairs and toward new adventures without her.

I did eventually get a motorcycle. It was an old 250cc Yamaha I bought for two hundred dollars from a guy in Pocatello, Idaho. I was living in Jackson, Wyoming for a summer during college, and so had to drive the motorcycle back over the mountains after handing over the money. While I was riding over Teton Pass at 8,000 feet a bee flew into my helmet, and as it buzzed and stung furiously at my face, I fumbled in a graceless and terrified effort to stop the motorcycle without flying off the side of the mountain. Because this happened within two hours of owning the bike, I very quickly developed a sour taste for riding motorcycles. I only owned it a month or two before it was sent off to a scrap yard, and what I mostly remember about riding isn't speed or power or flash. I remember feeling like the wind was going to tip me over on the highway, like I was about to crash into a rodeo arena packed with tourists because I couldn't quite steer the thing, and like I was always only moments away from a very painful death. When a mechanic pronounced the motorcycle's engine dead and the guy who sold it to me a crook, I expressed dismay but was secretly relieved.

On top of that, I'm clumsy enough to walk regularly into the side of door frames rather than through their wide openings, leaving my hopes of someday jumping through a ring of fire clearly out of the question. And I drive like an overly-cautious old lady, so I guess it's fair to say that I'm not exactly a lightning bolt motorcycle stunt person.

Still, recklessness has its place, and it comes in many forms. And I like to think that Derry would be proud if she could see me now. I suppose she'd be proud if she could see anything at all now, being made of plastic, as she is, and lying in the damp darkness under a pile of human garbage in some landfill in South Dakota, or wherever such toys go when thrown away.

While I've decided it's good to avoid mimicking Evel Knieval in my daily life, I'm still capable of the occasional death-defying stunt and still appreciate those toys. Life on a sugar high with a career, a family, a mortgage, and a Republican party gone mad is danger enough. Flying out third story windows and jumping over school busses can't possibly be more treacherous than this. I'm going shopping today, and I'm going to buy some brightly-colored plastic toys. Maybe they are for my kids. Maybe they are for me. I just think we ought to have some around.

I Did What I Could

If you could find my first grade schoolmates, and if you could somehow enhance their recall powers substantially, you'd find not one among those who played the sport who would disagree that I was the best floor hockey goalie in the entire grade. School was a confusing experience for me, but gym class was my anchor. I didn't struggle with actual school work, but the social world of elementary school was nothing if not complex, and for a girl who wore her identity right next to her nerves, on the outside of her body, a confusing social order could gum up the works.

In gym, though, everything was clear and I knew where I stood, and I stood in the goal for every floor hockey game. I was always one of the first players chosen if I wasn't doing the choosing myself—having become the gym teacher's most willing and enthusiastic assistant—and we almost always won. The great part was that, unlike less fortunate first graders, I had discovered something I was good at. I'd still be good at it if I could find a floor hockey league. I've got this weird ability to move very fast instinctively, trusting in my peripheral vision. Laid back people might live longer and enjoy life's riches more, well, evenly, but there are some activities at which we anxious people excel. For example, this particular skill now comes in handy when playing Whack-a-Mole at the State Fair. Or rather it would come in handy there, if they'd set the machines at a competitive pace. As it is, the pace of the moles popping up is so slow that even a non-gifted Whack-a-Moler can hit them all if he just concentrates a bit, so most games everyone finishes at the same time, and the system just chooses one of them randomly to be the winner. Shame, that. I'm not asking that it be a marketable skill, but I wouldn't mind if it came in handy for something.

Second grade teachers have a lot of power. A college teacher can be terrible, but her students will be fine or not, more or less, regardless of her ineptitude. A second grade teacher, on the other hand, can make or break a floor hockey career with a single mindless decision and a year's worth of bullheadedness. In June of 1972, Congress enacted and Richard Nixon, of all people, signed Title IX, an educational amendment that stated, "No person in the U.S. shall, on the basis of sex, be excluded from participation in ... any educational program or activity receiving federal aid." But these things don't take right away, and, three years following this particular act of congress, my second grade teacher Mr. Nelson, hadn't yet heard the news.

It was made clear to us at the beginning of second grade that gym was going to be the same as it had been the year before. It happened every day at the same time, and it was organized into two-week blocks, each block focused on a different activity so that we might develop skills and learn games without losing variety. The floor hockey weeks were the very best ones (there were entire blocks devoted to Duck, Duck, Gray Duck and, even worse, bowling, during which we spent 98% of our time resetting the pins by hand). When we played floor hockey, the time sped by so quickly I pouted something furious when it was time to go back to the classroom. Pouting, of course, is believed by many seven-year-olds to be a potent weapon, its utter failure in most cases notwithstanding.

We were several weeks into the year when floor hockey was finally due on the gym rotation schedule. I paid little attention in class the week before, as I murmured with my classmates about who would be on which team and engaged in some seven-year-old trash talk, which is nothing to laugh at if you're seven, let me tell you. On Monday morning, I chose my favorite clothes and headed off to school ahead of my older brother, who was supposed to accompany me to the school doors. I spent class time that day snickering, wiggling around, and avoiding eye contact with the teacher in hopes he wouldn't ask anything which might require that I'd been paying attention. This is another skill I was born with, again, not marketable but useful nevertheless.

At last, it was time for gym, the tiny but precious half-hour that was to be devoted to hockey each day for the next ten school days. The teacher asked us to put away the worksheets from whatever activity we had been engaged in and got up to stand at the door, the way he normally would when preparing to line us up and march us out. Then came the remarkable words: "Boys, I want one line in front of me. Girls, take out your crayons."

I managed to say something in complaint and whiny dismay, and he responded by refusing to look at me and simply repeating his instructions: "Boy's I want one line in front of me. Girls, take out your crayons." The *bastard!* Who did he think he was? I don't remember much more, but I do remember lying on the floor of my classroom and flopping all around as I screamed out in grief about that which was being denied me. I remember that the boys left with our teacher and that I was reprimanded and made to sit at my desk. And after that I remember endless fits at home, screaming about the inequity of the situation, the nerve of this sadistic teacher, the betrayal of it all.

As the days passed, each another half-hour of hockey lost, each another day with some other, less worthy kid in the goal, and each seeing no progress in my drawing ability, I tried to wage war. This meant that I pouted in school to the teacher who of course paid no attention to me, and at home tried to get my mother to take the guy to the Supreme Court of the United States of America. My mother did get involved, glory be, though she didn't take it as far as I thought she should have. It was always a good thing to have her on my side when I was apoplectic, as the alternative was unbearable and she really can be quite a force to be reckoned with. After getting off the phone with my teacher for the second time, she explained to me his bullshit position: "I realize Sara would be just fine out there with the boys, but the fact is that a lot of our girls would get hurt playing a game this rough."

Despite two weeks of my own efforts in the classroom and my mother's complaints in the office, we didn't win the battle. The floor hockey block ended, and the girls were told to stand up on that fresh new Monday, so that we could join the boys in the gym. Once there, we sat in a circle and began to take turns walking outside of the circle, patting each kid on the head before screaming "gray duck" and running, again, in circles. Wahoo. And worse, the boys now talked about floor hockey like it didn't involve me. It was over, just like that.

The rest of the school year was ugly. I got detention for the first time, and I got demoted to a lower reading group. We were called the Purple People Eaters, and everybody knew this was not something to be proud of. You can't cover up shame with a stupid name like that; the kids will see through it every time. In the spring, in a desperate plea to be noticed, came the final, humiliating blow. A boy in my class broke a finger in a soccer game, and he came to school with the finger splinted and bound with gauze. I wanted so much to be him that I came to school the next day with a popsicle stick wedged between my fingers and wet toilet paper molded around them, holding the popsicle stick in place. I held my hand gravely and looked the fallen athlete, so that all would know that this broken finger meant something very, very serious. It worked for about three minutes, and then Mr. Nelson came in. "Why do you have toilet paper on your finger, Sara?" Bastard.

So five years later when the same thing happened again, I was not about to let it go so easily. By then we were in Junior High, the only place one could go that might be considered worse than the second grade. Gym remained my saving grace, the thing I was best at and the only place where social confusion didn't rule. While everyone around me seemed to be moving proudly through puberty, my body and mind remained that of an ungendered kid. I didn't even begin my own awkward attempts at following gender norms until the eighth grade, when social pressure seemed to allow no alternatives. On the morning of picture day that year I actually tried to do the right thing. Two of the gender-appropriate girls, girls who would not usually bother with the likes of me, stopped me in the hall.

"What did you do to your hair?" the tallest and most confident one asked, caring not a whit for the pain inflicted.

Her friend poked her in the ribs with her elbow as if to call for at least some restraint, and said to the taller one, "*Duuuuhhh*, she tried to *curl* it."

In the seventh grade, though, I still believed that if I could just manage to wait until gym class, the rest of it would go away and I'd be fine. Here in junior high the organizational structure of gym class was more to my liking than it had been in second grade. There was a single gym, but it was massive, and there was a partition that could be extended to create two separate gym spaces. Still the curriculum was organized around two-week blocks of time, only now for each unit there were two different activities, and kids got the chance to select one of them before each unit began. Usually one activity was designed for those less apt to enjoy competition or serious movement (bowling remained popular here) and one was designed for the rest of us. Dodge ball, kick ball, track races, volleyball, and sit-up, pull-up routines were popular here. Floor hockey never did make it out of elementary school, where in my imagination it still rots in its boys-only stink hole.

Life went along pretty smoothly for a full half-year this way, and I was proud to be known again as a good choice for any team

(In my yearbook an imposing second grade boy wrote "Sara, You are the best girl dodge ball player. Doug," and you can tell from the worn edges of paper that I had an unhealthy attachment to this remembrance). And this time I was no longer alone as a girl. There were other girls who enjoyed sports much like I did. The level of their dedication, however, was to be determined one gray January Thursday, the day the next two new activities would be posted on the walls in the gym so that we could put our names in the appropriate boxes. And on that day, only two of us passed the test.

Joy Smolnik wasn't so much into sports as she was dignified, and she was not the sort of seventh grader who appreciated being told what to do. Joy was the class vice president, and she helped as a stage manager for the school plays. She paid attention in class and held no small degree of power in the social world centered in the hallways. She didn't have to do anything different to her hair on picture day, and her body had arrived in Junior High having already developed into that of a sizeable young teenager.

That Thursday I ran into the gym and tried to get near the front of the line at the sign up sheet, so as not to miss any of the day's activity (gym was still just a half-hour affair, while social studies, it seemed to me, went on for days at a time). When I got to the front of the line, though, there was no pencil taped to a string dangling there. There was nowhere to write my name. There was only another bullshit announcement. Under the usual heading of "Gym class sections," there were two columns. One said: "Girls: gymnastics," and the other, "Boys: wrestling."

Feeling the sting from Mr. Nelson poke its way through my skin yet again, I resolved to fight back, this time in a more organized, sophisticated, seventh-grade manner. And lucky for me, or so I thought at the time, Joy Smolnik wasn't taking it well either. While several girls complained, the boys, of course, were silent, though I didn't believe for a minute that this was because each and every one of them wanted to wrestle instead of doing summersaults or leaping over the vault. As Joy and I kept pressing the issue among our peers, however, even the other girls who complained fell away, resigned to work on the balance beam until the next round of choices came about. I could be pushed around pretty easily as a kid. I was terrified of the bus and elected to walk the two miles to school because of harassing kids who threatened to "kick my ass" every time I rode, and I could be counted on to laugh at the cool kids' stupid jokes. But gym, as I've said, was not a subject I could budge on.

We had only a week and a day to work with, as the activities were posted that far in advance, presumably to give the gym teachers time enough to prepare the equipment knowing how many students they'd be working with. Joy and I got active. We got our parents to call the school, and we both prepared our own letters of official protest, which we delivered, together, to the head gym teacher. Then we got crafty and circulated a petition declaring the practice discriminatory and demanding that all students be allowed to choose their gym activity. I got a handful of friends to sign it by cracking jokes and sending it to various slacker buddies via the personal note service during class, and Joy got other kids, the ones my method couldn't reach, to sign it by waiting until class was over and talking with them in the hallways. By the end of the next week, the gym teacher called the two of us aside for a meeting. We felt formidable, like we amounted to something, and we were proud that we had stymied the system sufficiently to force them to change their ways. The second grade this is not, I told myself, and I have become an older, wiser activist. I know how to make things happen.

Off to the side of the gym, the teacher leaned on a big piece of rolled up padding, and Joy and I stood there in our feminist glory, waiting for his submission. We won, he told us, and we would be allowed to wrestle, but there was something else we should know. Some of the kids had told their parents about our petition, and the parents were alarmed that boys and girls would be wrestling together, thigh to arm, buttocks to chest, that sort of thing. So the staff had concluded that the two of us could wrestle, but we'd have to wrestle only each other, every day, for two weeks.

This was an interesting victory. I wasn't at all sure that what I'd been fighting for was the right to wrestle, per se. I just wanted the right to choose is all. I didn't hold particularly strong feelings about wrestling, not like I did about dodge ball or kickball or chin-up routines. And while I felt I was a better athlete than Joy Smolnik, I was certain that she was fifteen pounds heavier than I was and that this wasn't going to go well for me.

I was quite right about that. Monday came, and the gym partition went up. The rest of the girls went to the gymnastics side, and Joy and I tried to look brave on our hesitant walk to the wrestling side. There was much snickering, as the pubescent boys felt the awkwardness of the situation too overwhelming to remain decent and respectful. So unsure were we of our victory that we found it difficult to act happy to be there, though turning back, we knew, was not an option now.

As I recall, we all sat around a wrestling mat, and one at a time, pairs wrestled. In rare moments we'd each be paired up to learn some move at the same time, but mostly we all watched as two others tugged and yanked and heaved. The gym teacher called out the pins and the take-downs and tried to explain how the matches were scored. One kid won, the other lost, and then they sat down while another pair was called into center ring. I know there are fewer and fewer gym teachers out there at all anymore, and that kids now are lucky to have gym once or twice a week, but this only makes my advice that much more pertinent: For god's sake, gym teachers, if they only get to be there for a half-hour, isn't there some way possible that they can avoid sitting down for most of it?

So there we were, Joy and I. Wrestling. After the first two days, once everyone saw how it was going to go and nobody was embarrassed to have girls there anymore, the snickering stopped.

We were just another boring wrestling match throughout which they tried hard to sit still and pay attention. I paid attention. I paid attention because every day, for ten days, Joy and I were called to the mat, sometimes starting with her on all fours, sometimes with me in that position, and every day Joy would yank my limbs and torso around until my back was on the floor, straining nearly ever part of my body, and then lay across my middle, squishing me across the stomach and chest so badly I couldn't catch my breath.

She'd stay there until the coach told her it was a pin, as if nobody could figure that out without his analysis, and he would often forestall this conclusion in order to point out some of the maneuvers Joy had used. So I lie there listening to him, thinking I was probably the only person listening to him, waiting to be released. I couldn't let on that I couldn't catch my breath, and I remember telling myself to *focus, focus, focus* on my breathing so that nobody could tell how much it hurt. When it was over, I'd find a spot as far outside of the circle as I could get and try to regain control of my lungs, or I'd stagger to the drinking fountain, holding my breath until I was far enough away to gasp openly for oxygen.

I never knew what Joy thought of the whole thing. Once it was understood that we'd have to wrestle each other, we stopped talking about it. My hunch is that she didn't enjoy heaving me around and lying there while being observed and analyzed any more than I enjoyed my part of it.

And so I'd just like to say to all those girls out there now who enjoy organized sports; to the twelve-year-olds who play on ice hockey teams and get ice time just like the boys; to the hundreds of thousands of girls riding in minivans to soccer tournaments that are organized, staffed, and gleefully competitive; to the seven-year-old girls who get to stand up and go to gym as often as their male counterparts; and to girls in every sport who take good coaching and fairness for granted, I'd like to say just one thing. Sure, brave and great athletes like Babe Zaharias, Wilma Rudolph, and Billie Jean King stood up to the demeaning affects of sexism to help fight for your right to be who you are, for your right to live in strong bodies and to know the pure joy of sport. Sure, Sojourner Truth, Abigail Adams, Susan B. Anthony, Patsy T. Mink, Alice Paul, and hundreds of other gutsy female leaders have been arguing on your behalf and taking crap for it for hundreds of years. But there are millions of us out there whose work also ought not be ignored. We weren't the great athletes. We weren't great leaders. We were just sweaty kids using what we had: the power of pouting, tantrums, and a lack of foresight so remarkable that we were willing to wrestle each other every day just to make a point. Community organizers, you might say. So even though I didn't testify before Congress or march on Washington, though I didn't write scathing columns condemning discrimination, beat Bobby Riggs in a televised match, or cross the north pole by myself, I did what I could. And you're welcome.

My Religious Education

Though surrounded by it at nearly every turn, I managed to learn absolutely nothing about religion while growing up. Luckily this lack did not interfere with my resolute belief that I knew everything there was to know about Christianity in particular and about all of religion in all times and places in general. Though adolescence provided me with a host of unsolvable mysteries, church was not one of them, as I decided by the age of fourteen that I had become an expert on all things religious.

My brother is three years older and five generations smarter than I am. He's got the kind of mind that things stick to whether he asks them to or not. My mind requires a bucket of superglue, reams of post-it notes, and unending repetition if a piece of information should harbor the aspiration to stick around up there for any amount of time. I recognized this arrangement when I was very young and decided to find my own way to move forward. Since I wasn't going to impress anyone or garner much attention with my memory or analytical skills, I opted for exploiting my own strength instead. And my peculiar gift has to do with being able to feel. I am the Einstein of emotions.

My brother can walk into a room and notice that the air ducts clearly connect to a forced-air heating system, which clearly means the house was built in the early 1920s since this block was developed decades earlier but then demolished in the late teens and rebuilt only five years later by a guy by the name of Chambers who introduced forced air systems to this city. How he always knows all of this, I have given up asking. He just does.

But I have my own talents. I can walk into that same room and know instantly that the guy in the corner is nervous, that the woman behind the counter is kind and honestly does hope we found the place without any trouble, and that my two-year-old will lose his composure in fewer than thirty seconds. I can be flooded with feeling too cold to focus on anything other than my toes, or too excited about the restaurant we will visit next to really listen to whatever's being talked about. I don't notice the air ducts.

My skin is of normal thickness, but my nerves don't live beneath it. They hover about two feet outside of my body, the antithesis of the force shields science fiction heroes wear to brave dangerous lands. If my brother was going to navigate the world by seriously, no kidding, knowing all about it, when I was eleven-years-old I decided instead that I would navigate my way by feeling all about it.

This decision to rely on my emotional gifts freed up my mind and my time tremendously. I decided reading books was not necessary in order to discuss them, paying attention or completing homework was not necessary in order to talk in class, and later, when I was old enough to get a job, that budgeting or counting money was not necessary in order to spend it. Instead, I proceeded through my early years with the sole aim not of understanding things fully, or really at all; my goal was to get a general sense of things and move on. I got a lot of very general senses about religion and churches, and this translated easily into my expert status. Since I wasn't out to intellectualize anything, strong feelings were tantamount to profound understanding.

My dad was a choir director and organist while I was growing up. He had an advanced degree in sacred music, and though that wasn't something any sane teenager bragged about, I held it close and let it confirm my deep roots in the world of the spiritual.

Despite the fact that the church he worked for and we went to wasn't necessarily Christian anymore—that had slipped away decades before my family got there—I still put my time in listening to organ and choir music, hanging out in churches, and just generally feeling the meaning of churches, and I thereby got the point.

My dad was forever practicing on our piano, and so even though I couldn't identify a single hymn by name or recite any of the lyrics (the choir didn't live with us, after all), I could hum twenty or thirty church songs without having to think about it much. Going to work with dad for a few hours meant sneaking into the minister's very own private office to steal sugar cubes from his coffee cart and leafing at whim through books in the church library when it wasn't even open. Having such a profound understanding of all things religious, and therefore having no need to actually read them, I'd handle the books as if overcome by profound memories of them, pretending that I was just checking to see that they hadn't been damaged in the church library and that they were available for the newer, less sophisticated readers who would certainly follow in my footsteps. It meant I could creep around the whole building by myself when few other people were around, and this in turn, coupled with my gifts, meant I knew the church like only a brilliant insider would.

On vacations, while my peers were riding roller coasters at Six Flags in Chicago or learning to water ski at some uncle's cabin, our very organ-loving and lefty churchy family would head west in the car and stop in small Midwestern towns to visit churches. We'd arrive while nobody else was there, my dad having arranged ahead of time to see and play the huge, wall-mounted instruments. We visited a church because the organ's mechanical action instruments were modern, or because the sanctuary's acoustics were famous in the field of organology. We did not visit a particular church because of its slant on Jesus. I don't recall that we ever even talked about that part of the equation, and this was likely due to the fact that the other three people in my family assumed we already knew the difference between Lutherans and Pentecosts and Baptists. It is equally likely that the difference was explained to me over and over again and that I was not listening. Once inside these churches, I had the same free rein I had in our own church while my dad worked in his office.

I would slide under the pews on my belly chasing or being chased by my brother, greet janitors like I was the newly-appointed visiting Reverend brought in from someplace impressive to enlighten the people, and preach with conviction to empty sanctuaries from the pulpits. I didn't offer any specific message in my sermons, but hollered out in incoherent sentences, my profound meaning made clear by my passionate tone. And almost always I could find their coffee sweeteners and load up to ensure that a good, uncontrollable sugar high would begin as soon as we were belted back in the car for another three-hour stretch of fighting over questions such as whether my leg was or was not over the line and whether or not my brother was singing specifically to torment me. And no, it is not just that I want to hurt his feelings or that it's boring; it really is torment and yes I know what that word means and I think I might pass out from the stress and can we please stop for a root beer float soon?

My expertise in Christian thinking was further enhanced at our final destination on these road trips, the primary purpose of which was to visit relatives in California. My grandfathers were both Christian ministers and their family lives revolved around the church. When we visited, there was always a lot of general talk about church, and it was naturally expected that we would go to church on Sunday mornings. This meant that every other year, I went to a minimum of two hour-long Christian services. An hour's worth of anything not involving sugar or overtly expressed foolishness was exasperating for me, and I behaved as if I'd been asked to wear a hair shirt and chant endlessly in Latin. Our own church at home didn't even have services in the summer time, and so in my mind we were vacationing at church-intensive summer camp.

When I was young enough to be in elementary school, these family-vacation church services were nerve-wracking. Since I didn't understand my intuitive gifts yet, I was made anxious by that which I didn't understand, and I didn't like going to other people's churches. We went in with no preparation at all, as if this was something anyone could do. And the minister or preacher would always welcome newcomers somewhere near the beginning of the hour, making me hope I wasn't alone. But immediately after the welcome was offered, my hope would disappear as the people all began to do seemingly random things in unison.

There was a never-ending dance of sitting and kneeling and standing and singing and reciting and walking to the front for the wafer or passing along the massive tray of tiny glasses of grape juice. My mother told me not to take the cracker or the juice, and I thought this a rotten deal. I was not interested in the tasteless wafer itself (I grabbed one every now and then because I cannot be told to leave a snack alone if there's a chance it might be sweet) but I did feel the sting of injustice regarding the drink. Grape juice was the only recognizably useful part of the hour.

My parents grew up in churches like these and when we visited our relatives they fell in step with the program like they'd never missed a Sunday. And my brother knew everything just because that's how his mind works and he never seemed surprised by things like this. Every time our family did something that we kids had never seen or done before, my brother would confidently participate, having somehow divined ahead of time just how things would go and just how the brighter child would behave when things went that way.

I'd sit crumpled over in the service, pulling on my earlobe, staring at some carved design on the pew, and mentally exploring my grandmother's Fresca collection on the door of her refrigerator when all of a sudden I'd notice that I was sitting by myself, exposed in my inattention to all in the rows behind us. I'd have to jump up startled and late and embarrassed because everyone else had spontaneously stood up at the exact same time a full thirty seconds before me. I'd glare at my brother standing confidently beside my parents, already two lines into a song I knew he'd never heard before. How did he know they'd all stand all of a sudden? He was forever reading programs and knowing everything and being irritating in this way.

I had only a few years of this difficulty to endure, however, because as soon as I decided to meet the world in my own unique way, I adopted a wholly new approach to Christian church services that helped me avoid embarrassment. My new plan did not, of course, involve paying attention, as such work was out of the question for one so gifted as myself. Since understanding the actual details was now not only undesirable but also unnecessary, I realized all I needed was a new game plan. As I still didn't pay attention to what was being said, I still stood up for hymns later than everybody else. But I learned how to bend the situation to my advantage.

As soon as I was jolted out of my daydreaming and became conscious that I was sitting and everyone else was standing, I'd grab the pew ahead of me with one hand as if for support, keeping my other hand on some part of my leg while standing up as slowly and deliberately as possible. This way everyone in the row behind us now staring at me would understand that because of my serious sports injury, I had to stand up very carefully. A good wince once my body was fully extended would solidify the gravity of my situation for all to see and fill me with an enjoyable degree of self-importance. In this way I turned an awkward and embarrassing situation into a beneficial one.

By attempting to get only the general feel of the service rather than get bogged down in its particulars, I learned other behaviors that made it easy to get by and avoid embarrassment. I learned that the Lord's Prayer was something one just came to know by heart if one lived in America and went to movies often enough. Hymns were easier to get through because I could take up the whole first verse with my leg injury dramatics and because I did finally come to understand that the words to the song were written in the book my mother had been holding open for me to see for years. If reading from the book was too much trouble, though, I could yawn excessively or bend down to tend to my injury and look at my watch in exasperation, as if I really did need to see my trainer soon for another round of grossly expensive laser surgery and could you people please move this along.

Eventually, I got pretty good at alternating between pretending I knew what was going on and pretending I had my own, more important things going on, and I concluded that I had this whole church experience figured out. Sure, I wasn't raised in a Christian church, but I got it. Once I learned how to get through the services, the ensuing boredom left me free to ponder other great questions of life during services. For example, each visit to California required much attention to figuring out where, if not in the white china bowl on the coffee table, Grandma was keeping the candy around the house.

Furthermore, there was the meal following the service to consider and, if one was lucky, manipulate. If the service was early, say nine in the morning, and if we went immediately to a restaurant with the family afterwards, the meal would likely be considered a brunch, and everybody knows that dessert is not a part of brunch. If we dallied at the church after the service, however, so that a hyperactive kid could play in the courtyard or because one of the kids could not be located, or if we were lucky enough to go to a later service, then the meal following church was far more likely to be a lunch, and everybody knows that dessert follows lunch.

If this part of my upbringing alone doesn't explain the true breadth of my understanding of religion at an early age, the Unitarian Church can take up the rest of the slack. After my parents turned thirty, they moved from California to Minnesota because my dad got a job offer there. They moved with two young kids thinking the stay would be temporary, and leaving most of their relatives in shock (Who leaves California? You're going *where*?).

And then, much to the surprise of the same people who thought it odd enough to leave the Golden State, these two children of mainstream Christian ministers joined a granola-eating, noncommittal, lacking-in-dogma, Unitarian church. This aroused deep suspicions in the more conservative branch of the family, one of whom accused my parents of moving to Minnesota to "be closer to those damned Kennedy's."

It turned out that my parents liked Minnesota a great deal and they stayed. My brother and I went on to spend years of Sundays as students in the Religious Education program at the Unitarian church. At the time, this RE program was like a broad but sporadic class in world religions. Since Unitarians are knit together not out of a shared creed but out of a shared desire to investigate spiritual and religious truths, at least in the winter, it's hard to come up with a label that fits all of them. They are agnostics and atheists, Christians of all stripes, Jews, and often times ex-Christians looking for a better fit. Unitarian ministers get the stuff of their sermons from all kinds of religious and spiritual traditions. We celebrate Christmas, yes, but for most of the year we keep the baby Jesus next to Odysseus and Mohammed, in myth rather than in our mouths via small shots of grape juice.

Knowing my unique form of knowledge came to me through simple emotional absorption, sitting in RE classes didn't require me to pay attention to what was being discussed. I was therefore free to screw off in the back of the room and find new ways to be obnoxious. What I absorbed, in the meantime, was an entirely random overview of what people in other places and times had to say about religion and god and the hereafter and how we got here and all of that. As I tuned in and out at whim while waiting for another opportunity to express my immaturity, other people in the room talked about different forms of religious practice.

They talked about Buddhism, Taoism, various Christian traditions, Judaism, Transcendentalism, and the varied histories of Native American and African American spiritual beliefs. I developed a vague feeling about each one, and let it go at that. And of course since vague feelings can be influenced by a host of factors at any given moment, my responses to the topics in class were dictated by the whims of no end of moodiness. If Buddhism came up on a day I felt particularly betrayed by my parents, I'd think of Buddhists as fascists who abused their power. Sure, they talked peace, but anybody could see it was nothing but a passive aggressive tactic used for control. If Native American creation myths were talked about on a day I felt the intensity of loss associated with not being born rightfully as one of the Supremes, I'd think of the animals that started it all as having messed seriously and injuriously with my fate.

Sometimes I'd take a liking to something. If we talked about the Transcendentalists, though I had no care in the world what the term meant, I felt empowered by my new plan to leave my parents and the identity of "daughter" behind, escape to the woods, do whatever I wanted to, and be considered by all to be doing something of serious importance.

The reason for this curriculum—to allow us to explore on our own and draw our own informed conclusions as we came of age— was entirely lost on me. I had no intention of coming of age, if that meant paying attention, and so for me, the message seemed to be a vague, "you now know an awful lot about religion; go forward and behave as if you knew of what you spake."

The daughter of an organist, the granddaughter of ministers, the product of years of progressive and broad religious education, I knew church. I was comfortable in conversations about religion, as long as the person I was talking to had no idea what we were talking about. For all others, I adopted a cynical snort which sufficed to indicate I knew all about it and didn't care to waste any more time talking about it, especially given the profound implications of the most recent and entirely imaginary MRI scan conducted on my right knee. A knowing, dismissive look accompanied by an indignant "humph" was the best and only dignity-saving response to a disagreement with my brother, who would prove himself utterly right and me utterly idiotic if a single coherent word was spoken.

When my junior high school teachers decided they had done what they could and that they didn't get paid enough to do anything more, they sent me onto high school, and my parents chose this pivotal moment in my life to change their policy on religious education. As I entered the ninth grade, they declared I could choose for myself whether or not to continue in the RE program at church. If a child chooses not to grow up on her own, some parents think giving them increased amounts of responsibility will help move the process along. My brother had chosen to stay. Since he listened and learned and therefore grew as a result, he found the program beneficial and fun. I waffled a bit. The antics in the back of the RE classroom were enjoyable, but I had never admitted to liking it and staying would blow my cover. In truth it was a short and serious girl named Cindy Perinsky who would make my decision about whether or not to continue in the program an easy and final one.

Every year Unity Church Unitarian produces a Christmas pageant that is known and beloved not because of its creative interpretation of the story in Luke, its stellar acting, its complex costume design, or, of all things, its affirmation of our beliefs about Christ. Our Christmas pageant is adored by hundreds of congregants for the simple reason that from year to year and decade to decade it never changes. The acolytes must walk up the center aisle in pairs, light the candles in an order decided upon I think in the 13th century, and fan out to the side aisles where they each take their predetermined posts under the windows that span the sides of the sanctuary. The heavenly hosts wear the same white gowns and feathery wings and follow their assigned angels the same way every year, and the shepherds stand on the very same steps to ponder the shocking words of the lord showing the same degree of no shock at all on their stony faces.

The ministers read the script from up in the balcony while the kids act it out in silent, minimalist fashion below. The angels approach Mary or Joseph or the shepherds each in turn, and to indicate they are speaking, they extend and raise one arm, pointing it up and out toward the character to whom the message of the lord is being directed. One year, the angel whose job it was to tell Mary that she was about to have God's baby and not to worry about that brought her arm down to her side not with the usual mechanical movement that she was told to use and that tradition demanded, but rather with a flourish of drama, a kind of swish that was almost elegant. Her chin jutted out while she did it, and she smiled, pleased with herself. The audience gasped. Women clucked their tongues. We were disgusted.

I think it's because few of us actually buy the story itself that we focus so heartily on the consistency of the performance. Since the tale of the manger and the star and all of it is a bit, well, tired, we've made a game out of the telling of it to keep ourselves interested. Each new director has to take a new batch of kids and maybe even new ministers and a new organist and produce something that is identical in every way to what was done in all years previous. If an angel were to come unto Joseph with the message that he should leave Bethlehem by the back road so as to avoid an angry king out to kill Jesus, if that angel should come into the sanctuary from the right instead of the left this year, I am quite certain hundreds would cry out in astonishment and at least half of the audience would leave that night promising not to return next year if they are going to let this foolishness go on.

Another of the two-hundred and thirty-seven traditions not to be messed with in the pageant is the tradition that holds that the roles of Mary and Joseph are to be played by high school seniors. This comes in handy as a way of persuading teenagers to stay in the church when their very genes scream at them to do something else with their Sunday mornings: Sure, you can leave and swagger around in coffee shops looking cool for the next four years, or you could stay here and we'll let you be the church equivalent of a rock star on Christmas eve. It's a surprisingly effective retention strategy.

At the beginning of my ninth-grade year, just before the year's first class in the RE program, Cindy Perinsky approached me outside of our classroom. Cindy and I had been in classes together for years, though we didn't know each other well, seeing as Cindy sat at the front of the room and listened and answered questions. I mostly recognized her by the back of her head and I understood and accepted the fact that she had little patience for the likes of me. So I had no idea what she might have wanted to tell me.

"I just want you to know," said Cindy, "that when we are seniors, *I* will be Mary."

"Mary?" I asked.

"That's right, Mary. I don't know who will play Joseph but Mary is mine. I want that to be clear."

I couldn't think of anything to say to that. Nothing at all. I looked one last time into the room I had intended to walk into, and then went upstairs to wait for my parents next to the sugar cubes and coffee. When they emerged from the service an hour later, I informed them that I had made my decision and was hereby finished with church school.

If sitting in the front and paying attention to what was actually being said were going to be rewarded, and I sensed as I sense best that they were, then Cindy Perinsky and all the others like her were going to win. Clearly, this was an institution that didn't appreciate my gifts. What I needed, I decided, was a place where deeply held feelings were appreciated far more than ideas or concrete bits of information. I needed a place where those who basked in unearned glory got the all of the attention; where those who felt deep pain and sorrow could convince others immediately of their own importance; and where adults with reason and control over their emotions had so little power or respect that their insights would not be heeded. All I needed started the very next day at 7:20 in the morning. On that day, I attended my first day of public high school, and with that my decision to skip the rest of church school was affirmed. I had experienced all of the church that would be necessary, thank you, and was moving onto the next stage of my life.

Shrink Wrap, Diet Cokes, and a Kazoo

The only thing about the roughly nineteen part-time jobs I held between the ages of fifteen and twenty that allows me to say they were, at times, amusing, is that I don't hold them anymore. There are jobs that ask so much of a person she thinks she might die, and there are jobs that ask so little of a person that she thinks she can't die soon enough. The pay is often the same.

Throughout summer vacations during high school and college, I'd often sign on at local temp agencies. This allowed me to have both a flexible schedule and really terrible work options. Most of my jobs were in factories, and there I saw the manufacturing and packaging underbelly of American culture, which, as far as I could tell, is about 10% manufacturing and 90% packaging. I worked on many assembly lines, usually putting shrink wrap of varying thickness around all sorts of products before sending them into machines that heated them, causing the wrap to shrink (so that you can best appreciate what you have, remember next time you struggle to open a plastic-coated product and curse the need for pliers and industrial-strength scissors that they do it this way because it's cheap, easy, and highly wasteful).

Once, moving up from packaging, I worked for a short time at a factory whose primary purpose was to spray chrome plating onto plastic car decals. My fascinating and useful task there was to clip hundreds of variously-sized, molded Thunderbirds onto huge racks, which were then wheeled by somebody else into a paint room. I never saw the finished product, I suspect because that would have given me a sense of satisfaction, if slight, at having accomplished something, and that's something most factory designers clearly work hard to avoid.

For another job, I was given orders to appear at what I was told was a printing factory, where the man who would be my supervisor for the next nine hours met me in a sad little lobby. He directed me to follow him, and we set off into a vast room filled with massive, loud, and very impressive looking machines. Most of them were the size of vans, and some were as big as a small one-room cabin. Their controls consisted of huge levers and big, red and white buttons that no sane person could resist pushing. They made fantastic powerful whirring and chopping noises, and I wondered if they ever rented the place out for birthday parties. While we passed through this room, the supervisor yelled a question at me over the roar of two machines nearby that were cutting thick stacks of paper with blades bigger than my hatchback parked out on the street.

"You ever collated before?"

"Gosh no, but I can learn really fast," said I, wide-eyed. Who thinks to look up words like "collating" in the dictionary?

I was excited, anxious to see how big my machine was going to be, and wondering whether I too would get to wear safety goggles and thick working gloves. Then my supervisor and I approached a wall at the back of the cavernous room, against which there were paper-sized slots, like mailboxes in an employee break room. Each box was filled with two inches of paper of assorted colors. Beneath those, at about waist level, was a shallow counter. I looked at the other people facing the wall and quickly worked up a panic. There would be no machines, big or otherwise for me, and there would be no need for goggles here. No way, I thought. All *day*?

My only piece of equipment was a disc of red goo in which I was instructed to rub my fingers whenever they lost the stickiness they needed to quickly grab a sheet of paper. I was to reach up and take one sheet of paper from the top box, one from the second, and so on, working my way down until I had a completed stack of ten. I was to count the number of stacks up to fifty, put each pile of fifty into a box, and repeat the process until the bell indicated it was break time. That was it. The great machines roared away at my back, but I couldn't even turn to watch for fear I'd lose track of how many stacks I had in my pile.

Non-temporary employment, I discovered, didn't offer a great deal more stimulation. The biggest difference between most of these jobs and the temporary factory jobs is that in non-temp jobs you knew right when you got up in the morning how much your job would suck. As the only employee on duty most of the time at a seldom-visited fast food restaurant in a mall, I rarely kept busy frying and microwaving and making change. More often I did the required prep work, which was broken down into seven steps on a three-foot high, large-print poster in the back, and then stood behind the counter with not a thing to do, ruing my mundane plight.

On one particularly slow afternoon, after several minutes spent shifting my polyester visor from one side of my head to the other for variety's sake, I leaned over the counter, and rested my head on my hand. I stared off into space and felt the full weight of the exasperation my boredom evoked. Then I espied a strange couple approaching me. At first I thought the one on the left was a fragile old woman, because she was stooped over and weak, and the hulking man on the right held her arm to steady her as they walked ever-so-slowly toward my counter. But as she got closer and my eyes remembered how to focus, her clothes betrayed her. She wore trendy teenager clothes, which, it being the 1980s, meant that she wore a bright pink polo shirt with the buttons unbuttoned and the collar sticking up, stonewashed jeans that were rolled and tucked tightly around her ankles, and bright white Reebok high-tops with laces and Velcro straps. This was no old lady. It was a Cindy Lauper, Boy George, M.C. Hammer-lovin' teenage girl, probably about the same age as I.

As they approached, I read all the signs. She was weak because she was so very skinny that her skeleton jutted out. Below the hem of her sleeve I could see both bones in her upper arm, and she wore a hospital bracelet on her wrist. The hulking man I assumed to be her father walked and spoke to her in a manner suggesting he was tense and frustrated. I felt hopeful and self-important, because I was sixteen and therefore had two primary responses to all situations: I oversimplified all things and considered them only in so far as they concerned or featured me. My reasoning in this case was that since my restaurant didn't sell anything I could think of that had fewer than 600 calories per serving, I could do something useful.

Up at the counter, and without making eye contact with me, the girl whispered an airy,

"Ah … ha … sma die co, plee."

"I'm sorry, I didn't hear you," I said.

Then she firmed up a bit and looked at me, and gave it another try. Though soft, the voice was clear this time: "I'll have a small diet coke please."

"Sure," I said, deflated.

I was just turning around when the man holding her elbow exhaled loudly, thumping his other fist on the counter. I froze and looked back at him, hopeful that he'd add something to the order, demand a baked potato with imitation sour cream and baco-bits, a large fries, and a lard-based milkshake. And in a tiny, useless way, my hopes were realized, as he did, indeed, add to the order. His chest was puffed out and he bellowed his demand slowly, annunciating each word with care:

"Medium. She'll have a *medium* diet coke."

And then he slapped a five-dollar bill on the counter as if to suggest that he'd pay for four medium diet cokes if he could get her to drink them. I filled the order, sticking the cup under the regular coke spout for as many seconds as I thought I could get away with, and wondered helplessly what else I could throw in before putting the plastic cap on the top. If only I'd had the foresight to stick a few corndogs in the blender before this pair got here. The customers made their slow, trembling way toward a bench to sit down and work on the beverage, and I went home at the end of the day, aware that on that day my job was as close to meaningful as it was ever going to get.

I'd have stayed longer at any of these jobs, though, would have kept clipping car decals, collating papers, and pouring diet cokes, if I could have avoided one half-hour-long bowling alley job I stumbled through sometime in high school.

For a few years, I worked for a guy who owned a balloon store. We sold stuffed animals, gift bags, spinning tops, plastic rings, and balloons. I worked regular hours in his store, and during festivals, I walked around selling individual mylar balloons for three dollars each. The people who bought balloons were almost always in pleasant moods, something you can't say about your typical shrink-wrapper, so the job was pretty painless. Soon after I started working at the balloon shop, the owner decided to expand his business by adding balloon deliveries to our repertoire, and I jumped at the chance to make more money for what seemed to be little work. He had an old gorilla suit lying around and then scraped together cheap and minimal costumes for the other two characters he thought most likely to sell. Since I knew how to juggle, he bought a clown's wig and suit, and he figured a cowgirl would be discernable if he invested a few dollars in a hat and vest. So, people wanting to hire me got to choose a clown who juggled, a gorilla who played Happy Birthday on a kazoo, or a cowgirl who did nothing but hand off the balloons and leave.

The deliveries were not comfortable affairs, generally, and they didn't get better as time went by; the clown always made kids cry, and, having no idea what to do about that, I'd just start juggling, count silently to twenty, and then leave, yelling out "Happy Birthday" over the screams and parental coos and hushes. The cowgirl was awkward because she had nothing to do or say, and I was incapable of coming up with a "Howdy y'all," schtick. So I handed off the balloons, counted to five, and then left saying nothing, feeling the kids' stares and the parents' sting of wasted money at my back. At first I appreciated the gorilla suit above the others, because the mask hid my discomfort. But gorilla suit deliveries had their disadvantages too.

The biggest problem was that the suit itself was made for a very large man, someone a foot taller than I was. There was no danger of it falling off, but I could hardly move in the thing. The pant legs were so long that I had to roll them up several times to keep them above my shoes. They unrolled easily, though, and when that happened, walking normally was impossible. I tried many forms of walking in this condition, the most successful of which was a kind of dragging shuffle that required neither foot to leave the ground, but I still found myself sprawled over doorways, front steps, and couches on many a delivery.

The hands of the gorilla suit were not rollable, and so hung down another six inches from my hands, making the gorilla appear to have two severely broken arms and making me have to grab balloons, keys, and doorknobs through the thick synthetic fur. More problematic was that the mask was so grossly huge that the eye and mouth holes weren't anywhere close to my own eyes or mouth. And if I held the mask so that the gorilla's eyes matched up with mine, its mouth was still a good inch too low. Who has a face this big? If I could not hold the mask with both hands in order to see, because, for example, I needed one hand to hold a bunch of balloons, the eye holes rested much further south, roughly parallel to my nose. My vision, therefore, was entirely limited to the two foot wide by four foot high area directly in front of my feet. I could not look to the side, for the mask did not turn when my head did, and I could neither look straight ahead nor up. And then there was the kazoo problem.

The kazoo given to me to perform my duties was a wee bit larger than the plastic mask hole into which it needed to fit. So I'd have to cram it in there using both of my hands, which were themselves struggling to feel the kazoo at all through the bunched-up gorilla suit sleeve. The kazoo-cramming exercise was so awkward and left open so big an opportunity for crude jokes that I often elected to do it before entering the house or restaurant. So I'd park the van, hide behind it to roll up the pant legs in hopes of staying on my feet, stick the kazoo in the mask and the mask on my head, fumble for the balloon strings through the sleeve of the suit, and trudge toward the door, looking only at my feet. I'd get there based on memorized details I'd gathered while still in the van: five steps to sidewalk, turn right, feel for railing, door to left. Watch for thick doormat.

One night I was told to make a gorilla delivery at a bowling alley in a suburb I'd never heard of before. The bowling alley was huge—from the outside it looked like a super-sized grocery store. I felt like I was in a different world altogether, as it had never occurred to me that this many people on the entire planet went bowling. I parked in the busy parking lot and wondered how the hell I'd get inside since the distance from my van to the entrance alone was longer than any distance I'd managed to walk in the gorilla suit before. I was also acutely aware of the number of teenagers roving around the rows of cars and congregating and the main entrance, and I cursed the lack of privacy available for my costume change and for balloon deliveries in general.

The parking lot was thick with slush, and my rolls of pant legs were soaked by the time I made it to the door. The kazoo sticking out of my mask led the way; my eyes, of course, peered down, and I groped for the door handle while shrinking from the teenage snickering that surrounded me. Once inside, I felt the vastness of the building and considered my next move. My instructions told me to find lane thirty-seven, where a party was being held for a man named Kevin. I was to find Kevin, hand him the balloons, and kazoo him his song.

Thirty seven is a lot of lanes, and as I couldn't look up, or even out, I didn't know exactly how I would be able to identify lane numbers. So, I shuffled down the crowded lobby area at an angle. I kept my body just sideways enough so that I could count the number of bowling-ball return racks as I moved, since I could see the sloping bottoms of them where they touched the waxy floors. I couldn't see what people were doing, but I heard their conversations stop as I approached, and I felt their stares. When I got to the lane I figured was within five lanes of Kevin, give or take, I stopped and wondered what to do. People were talking about me, but nobody spoke to me to give me any direction ("Oh my god!" "What is that supposed to be?" "What's wrong with his arm?" "Is he drunk?"). I don't know why people think it acceptable to talk about gorillas right in front of them. Do they think we don't have ears? We do, and the holes work fine thank you, even if they are not always in just the right spot.

I wanted to ask for Kevin, but the kazoo was wedged in my mouth hole. Since most deliveries took place in living rooms, I was not used to having to pick a balloon-recipient out of a mass of hundreds of random people. So, failing to come up with other options, I figured the gorilla's nostril holes had to suffice, and I murmured, "Is this Kevin's birthday party?" with as much enthusiasm as I could muster, which was not enough to be measurable or even, apparently, heard.

Nobody responded, that I could tell, so I stood there looking at the floor a while longer, hoping whoever the hell had ordered me would stand up and take charge of the situation. How could anyone miss this slumped over, broken-armed gorilla with a kazoo wedged into its mouth? Finally, thinking I'd die there if I didn't do something, I stammered out a louder, "WHERE"S KEVIN?"

through the nostril holes, and a woman's voice did, at last, acknowledge me. She took me by my gorilla sleeve and directed me to where I could see the belt and legs and shoes of Kevin. I held out my left arm to deliver the balloons, the left hand of the gorilla dangling below, parallel to the balloon ribbons. I held the balloons with a very tight fist for what I hope by now are obvious reasons. I could not see the actual hand-to-hand transaction because that took place well above my line of vision, so there was some struggle involved before Kevin's legs could communicate to me that he had them, thank you, and please let go.

During this struggle, I said nothing, as my only plan for further expression involved the kazoo, and for that I needed my hands free. Noting that the slew of balloon ribbons hanging in front of the legs of Kevin stayed there, facing me, and noting the obvious hush of expectancy all around me, including even a lack of thuds from bowling balls hitting the floor and ball-to-pin crashes, I understood that the time had come to perform.

Preparing to kazoo involved tilting the gorilla mask upward so that my mouth could make contact with the kazoo. This was, by the way, the only time in costume that I was able to look up, since the eye holes, if the mouth hole was in the right place, were about an inch higher than my eyes. This meant my visual memories of all gorilla deliveries were limited to details of flooring, stairs, and the legs and feet of people, and a few quick glances at ceilings. There at Kevin's birthday part, my lips groped in the darkness for the back of the instrument, and I commenced kazooing.

As I kazooed, I thought of several things other than the song itself or Kevin's happiness. I tried to focus, out of necessity, on holding the gorilla's face up toward the ceiling so that I could blow on the instrument. But while doing this, I became aware that I was standing on one leg of the gorilla suit. It had come unrolled during the balloon hand-off and was now irretrievable. And, unable to see anybody, even anybody's shoes, staring up as I was, the social mortification that began in the parking lot leapt to new, unchecked heights, and I imagined the body postures and facial expressions that must surely have surrounded me, all of them showing disgust at my ineptitude, and at least one of them showing appropriate fury at how much she'd paid to have to endure this. I was nearly paralyzed with a desire to be anyplace else. As is well known in balloon delivery circles, it takes a lot of air to get your typical kazoo to boom like it was meant to, and I was too defeated to muster enough, so about half of my rendition of "Happy Birthday" came out kazooed, and half came out as indiscernible airy passages.

When it was over, not that anybody would have known whether it was over or not, I noted the relative silence of the place, thought of my usual nothing to say, and so pivoted around on the dangerously entangled leg to face the long path leading to the exit. Since readjusting my pants was impossible without taking my mask off, and since there was no way in hell I was taking my mask off, I settled for dragging that leg and its undignified train over the carpet and eventually through the slush, until I could sling the whole thing violently into the back of the van. The walk out of the goddamned bowling alley felt far longer than the by-no-means-brief walk in, and as I moved I watched hundreds of legs and feet, all facing me, part to the sides, making a path for my solitary, limping, and dragging retreat. I peeled out of the parking lot as fast as the slush would allow and sped home indignant and humiliated.

When I become president and grand poobah, the first item on my agenda will be to create and christen a new branch of government, something called MERA, the Meaningless Employment Regulatory Agency. They'll monitor the worst low-paying jobs and make sure of two things: that everyone has one for a short time and that nobody has one for long. And I know just where I'd house the hundreds of full-time employees who would staff MERA. In Washington DC there is an official-looking five-story building a few blocks off the mall on G Street, a building that takes up more than half a city block. Out front is a sign, declaring the building to be the "Government Accountability Office." Since this building is obviously not currently being used for a damned thing, I would move MERA in immediately and order a corresponding sign to replace the one now there, so that passersby would no longer fall to the ground laughing, scuffing even their non-gorilla pant legs and spilling their drinks. Once MERA is up and running, everyone will look forward to the day when they can look back and laugh at the work they once did, because as I said, it's not funny until you're not doing it anymore.

Precious

My favorite thing about massive wealth is the limitlessness it promises, at least in the fantasies I entertain for a minute or so most times I pass by the lottery billboard on my way home from work. I see the daily total, now standing at $122 million, and I think first of the immediate stresses in my life: the plastic cover on the light inside my minivan, the one that won't stay taped up for more than a day and keeps dangling there. Or what I'd have for dinner, if I could go anywhere and afford anything. I think about good food a lot. I think maybe I could pay some teenager to fix that fencepost in the back yard that bows ominously, threatening to yank the whole side of the fence to the ground, or that maybe I'd call the garage door guy and get him to really fix the thing. Then I wouldn't have to fidget with those little laser beam gadgets on the sides of the door that never seem to want to keep looking at each other, and so turn away from one another as if in an argument, consequently telling the garage door to come down when I push the button, but not all the way down, and then to come back up and stay there, defying my button-pushing commands. Hell, I might not even have the guy fix those laser things. I might buy new ones. But mostly I think about that damned plastic cover hanging down from the light in the van. It irritates the crap out of me, and I'd really like to drive to the dealer and get it fixed. No haggling about price either. Money is really a bother not to have.

Still, the truth is that there exists the occasional person who can use wealth to make the world seem bigger for everybody. Annie and Peter were friends of mine in college. They were lovers, adoring one another beyond the bounds of a typical college romance. They were also mighty rich, Peter coming from a prominent Massachusetts advertising family and Annie coming from an old-money Virginia family.

Peter was a brilliant and passionate man and Annie adored him, rolling with his various and constantly changing passions like only a devoted lover could. One month his would be a passion for architecture, the next for photography, the next for sustainable living in the mountains, always for Annie. His declared major would change, as would his plans for graduate school, and his investments in new magazines and organizations. He never did anything half heartedly, and his family supported his shifting career ambitions. He could make anyone believe in the brilliance of his new plans, and his parents faithfully went along, writing more checks each time the plans changed.

I loved Annie and Peter, because at a time of great discomfort and no small degree of despair on my part, hanging out with them meant living with abandon and a level of enthusiasm usually seen only in the very naïve or the very high. Whatever they did, they thought it the very best thing they'd ever done. When we went out for Mexican food, they ate with such wonder and joy, and used phrases like "I think this is the *best* enchilada I've *ever* tasted" all the time. Their eyes would grow wide at times like these; they would yell in the excitement of their new discovery and order another margarita. I would too. If other patrons sat close enough, they'd be swept into it too, and we would all leave believing we were anointed with elite information: We knew of this very special place, just outside of town, one not many people know about that honest to god served the best damned enchiladas ever made.

A few years after college, driving around the country in a 15-year-old pick up truck and camping where I could, I visited the two of them. Peter was on a tear about liquid-only diets. These would clear the bodily system of toxins, he announced, and make a person feel so good Peter couldn't believe how great it was. They each had weekly enemas (though Annie was noticeably less enthusiastic about this part of the plan than Peter) and talked endlessly about the thousands of combinations they could blend for meals. Peter always looked like he'd just discovered sex when he talked about these obsessions. He'd love each of them, of course, but he was such a good man, a caring man, that he desperately wanted you to love them too, to understand the joyous profundity of this new way of life.

They'd been on this kick for months by the time I visited, and had gone through several high-end juicers in search just the right model. Some were too inconvenient, some the wrong color for their kitchen. They gave me one they had discarded in a garage because it made a noise they found off-putting. I came home and set up my new juicer, so sure of this new system that I consumed only smoothies for four or five days. I was seduced, as always, by Peter's enthusiasm and his meticulously researched conclusions, and so it was with utter surprise that I greeted my saner friends' deductions when I announced that I was having considerable trouble with diarrhea. I put my juicer away and ate a sandwich.

I never saw Peter when he was coming off of one of these highs. I'm not sure he ever hit a low, gripped his stomach, and cried out at his own insanity. Each of his pleasures was simply overtaken, eventually, by a greater joy, and the juicers would slowly disappear while more solid food made its way into the kitchen. Annie eventually slowed her enema schedule, and then stopped it altogether without much conversation.

Anyway, these two got married when we got out of college, and they asked me and many other friends to be in their wedding. I thought it would be great—a chance to visit Nantucket, which I could not otherwise afford to see. There would be foolish outfits maybe, but I could bear it, I thought. Though ever-uncomfortable in college, these two could make me forget it, and I was delighted to have a chance to spend the weekend with them.

I had good reason for being uncomfortable. At my college, one that costs as much as the Ivies but doesn't require quite the same strenuous academic preparation, I was surrounded by New England money and Manhattan money (I heard enough to know that these are different categories, but I couldn't tell you why), by people who declared in liberal arts classes that they valued above all else making a lot of money at whatever human cost and had the financial support and privilege to go on and do just that, by people who shopped only on 5th Avenue, inhaled unbelievable amounts of cocaine, took exotic vacations over spring break, and boarded their polo ponies at our school. Because of their preparatory educations at Philips Exeter and Andover, whatever those places are, they also almost always knew the answers to the questions our professors asked in class and managed to turn in fairly decent assignments, sometimes even whilst wiping the blood from their cocaine-saturated noses.

There were normal people there too; I know because I would not have survived the four years without deep and honest friendships with people who could either guffaw louder than I at, or simply ignore, the madness we found ourselves immersed in. But generally, I hated it. I came from civil servant parents and clergy grandparents, from a midwestern city, a Unitarian church, and a public school seeping with liberal, middle-class values. My high school English class of 40 students took a survey after Reagan was elected for a second time, and we discovered that only one kid among us had one parent who had voted for the man.

Why I chose this college is an idiotic story for another day, but it wasn't what they call a good fit. I didn't dress well and failed to show any signs of promise in this area. Only a few years before going to college I was at a friend's house and saw her sister preparing to go to her senior prom. I told her she had a beautiful dress. She said it was her slip, and walked out of the room to get away from me. I certainly didn't have the money that so many of my peers had. I really believed, no kidding, that our purpose in the world was to make it a better place for others, had never seen a polo or lacrosse game or known anyone who went to a boarding school, and considered the epitome of spring break the opportunity to drive all the way to the Florida Keys in an overheating Ford Escort, with just enough money for a campsite and a few days of food. Still, Annie and Peter didn't care about any of it. They had money, but they paid little attention to its presence or rare absence and spent their time adoring one another, enjoying their friends, and blustering forth about the wonders they discovered.

The wedding was a three-day event, all of it catered, fully scripted, expensive beyond anything I could have imagined. This wasn't, much to my chagrin, due to Peter and Annie's enthusiasm for a good time or disregard for cost. Even their zeal was overshadowed by that of their parents, to whom this weekend clearly belonged. I was in no way prepared for what followed after I got off the ferry.

As the official wedding party (as if we were a breathing, portable fiesta) we were herded here and there, sent from one preplanned activity to another, everything prepared before our arrival. Peter and Annie are many things, but scripted is not one of them. They go where the winds tell them to go, and they go there fully, with ecstasy and no trace of regret. This was something wholly different. But they approached it the same way they did everything else, with pure astonishment and glee, like they had just stumbled onto Nantucket and found the best damned wedding they'd ever seen. Each sip of a new merlot brought them to the same state the enchiladas always did.

But for me this was very different than finding the greatest Mexican food in the world in a little place across town in upstate New York. I guess being told you're having a fabulous time isn't as effective as finding it where nobody expects it to be. For three days every time my cup was half empty, a uniformed man would be there to fill it up. They stood behind us, these reserved people in uniforms, looking a lot better than I did and never so far away that they would miss a drink getting past the half-empty mark, or the opportunity to pull a chair out in order to assist a person in the act of standing up. If I asked for something new—a beer, for example, or a cup of tea—the response was always the same: "Certainly. What kind would you like ma'am?" "What kinds do you have?" I would ask, thinking myself in a normal situation. The server would laugh tensely at me, visibly reddened by the insult, and say in a firmer, slower, and much quieter voice, "No ma'am, what kind would you like?"

I was told two days into the event that if they didn't have what someone ordered, another person was sent to town or the mainland forthwith to procure it. After that I ordered things I was certain they had, a brand I saw someone else drinking or something so common they at the very least wouldn't need a boat to get it. I started drinking only Budweiser when given the chance. At other times, the more formal moments for which the champagne or wine had been chosen in France months before, I just held out my glass and said "thank you." There were lavish tent parties on the beach, formal dinners in fancy and very old homes, bicycle rides on meticulously groomed, paved trails with people wearing a whole lot of linen (it was hard to remember that I was not in a J. Crew catalogue, but somehow also comforting to realize that those ads are not entirely artificial in their representation of reality), and rides in London Taxis, the cars that Peter's family had ferried over to the island just for the occasion (ferried from where, I never had the heart to ask, but I like to hope that Boston has a healthy stock of them on the ready for occasions such as this and am quietly assuming that they were never actually in London itself).

Most other wedding party members, and certainly the families and guests, knew exactly what to do with all of this, and I tried to learn quickly. Nearly the only thing I learned, however, was that this kind of money could be so constricting as to threaten a person's ability to breathe normally. I noticed that the women spent a lot of their time gasping, at the decorations in a room, at someone's dress, shoes, ribbons, hair—you name it—and clasped their hands together in front of their chests as if each hand needed to grab onto its companion in order to comprehend a moment of such aesthetic perfection. Sometimes this gesture would be followed by an extension of these same hands to meet and clasp the equally extended hands of the woman being congratulated for her choice in ensemble or decoration or whatnot. Then the two bodies would go rigid, sometimes on tiptoe, before seeming to collapse into a double-cheeked kiss. The men clapped each other on the backs a lot and stood at the periphery talking about I know not what when they weren't just behind and to the side of the gasping women. The men did not express astonishment; that clearly was not their job. And after seeing enough of it, it occurred to me that though the women were absolutely genuine in their joy when they saw, for example, yet another lavish floral arrangement, they were used to this and good at it and knew just what to do. What they were genuine about was the role they were playing, this weird game of gender and money and show, not the tulips.

The day of the wedding was the most heavily scripted of all, though because of this, I had the least idea what to do with myself. We bridesmaids (seven of us, including the bridesmaid supreme or whatever the hell she's called) had an entire historic house that was rented for us for the dual purpose—these people are nothing if not efficient—of providing a place in which we would first dress ourselves, and then dress the bride. Nobody even slept in the house, that I know of, and the rooms in which we dressed were decorated to appropriate clasping, gasping levels. We were driven to this house with all of our baggage; mine a neatly packed duffle bag and the garment bag insert from an old suitcase for my dress, *four hours* before the wedding. We weren't eating there, or riding bicycles, or drinking. We were getting dressed.

Now I understand the cultural and psychological importance of rituals, and I understand there are times when we ought to dress nicely. It's fine with me, even if I'm not very good at it, that we try to look pleasant when honoring significant events. But there is no reason in hell that I will ever need more than twenty minutes to get dressed, and in all of the years that I'd known Annie, I never knew her to need assistance getting her own body fully and appropriately clad. And there is no dress that is necessary to human progress that requires that a woman have not just help but the help of seven other women to put it on. Anyway, there we were, in the set of rooms prepared for our preparation, and the other women went right to work. So I put my bag down and did the same.

I took off my clothes (1½ minutes, tops), pulled on the ivory nylons purchased for us in Europe (2-3 minutes; I'm not so good at that—I get them all the way up, realize the crotch is down by my knees, and then have to start over), slipped the dress over my head, my feet in the dyed, size-ten slippers, and stuck a hat on my head (total: less than 6 minutes). When I looked up to figure out what to do with the remaining hours, hoping to get a cue from some of the other women, I noticed that none of them was moving perceptibly past step one. One was doing something to her toenails (the slippers did not show our toes), one was in what I by then knew was a slip doing something very intricate with her lips, her head thrust so close to the mirror that it looked as if she were making adjustments to a kiss. Others were ironing their already-ironed dresses or intensely focused on their hair, paying no mind to the fact that we were to wear hats for the duration of the ceremony. It takes me more time to put on jeans, a knit shirt and laced shoes than this one-piece outfit and slippers required. The dress didn't even have clasps or zippers or buttons in the back for which one might require additional time or assistance. You just threw it over your head and let it fall. Done.

The outfit was my least favorite part of the entire weekend, and I knew coming over on the ferry that this was the part that I'd just have to suck up. So you get the full effect, I can describe it from top down. We wore straw hats trimmed with pink ribbon (purchased by one of the mothers in France—what's the deal with France? I kept wondering) that trailed down our backs and was cut at the ends at a precise angle. I had heard no fewer than three conversations about this angle already over the course of the weekend. We wore pink ribbon necklaces, given to us by the bride. I'd put mine on in the morning so as not to lose it—unfortunately one less thing to kill time with that afternoon. We wore pink linen dresses from Laura Ashley, then the nylons and the slippers, which were dyed to precisely match the Laura Ashley dresses. I felt like a bottle of Pepto Bismol. Even Barbie doesn't wear this much pink at one time, and Derry Daring would at the very least have put a sparkly lightning bolt right up the middle.

So I stood there in the center of the room, trying to figure out what everyone else was doing and realizing with no small amount of anxiety that I was to be alone in my boredom for the next several hours and an outsider for the duration of the trip, when the supreme bridesmaid, the one in charge of the rest of us, swirled around from her lip-care work and saw me standing there. The gasp came first, which hushed the rest of the room. Then the hands came together, and I understood that I was to be subjected to the very same treatment I'd seen so many hairdos and outfits and flowers get. She sucked in her breath and her body went rigid and everyone turned around. She stared at me, this woman I didn't know, the woman most comfortable in this strange world I was visiting, and while finally allowing herself to exhale, said so that all might hear and see and understand, "She's *precious!*"

In the thirty seconds or so that followed, I stood paralyzed, aware of the sudden intensity of the oohs and aahs in the room; someone not in my line of vision started fidgeting with the back of my hair without disrupting the hat, as if she had been given

permission, all of a sudden, to adjust various aspects of my person. Bridesmaid supreme, thank god, had not followed through
with the full ritual of coming to grab my hands and kiss my cheeks,
but stood at a distance, as a florist might stand back to admire his
bouquet.

I think it was the third-person pronoun that sent me over the
edge. I wonder whether I'd have been able to stand it if she'd just
made the simple adjustment that grammar and the
acknowledgement of my humanity require and said, "*You* look
precious." But I can't say. She didn't. More objectified than I'd
ever felt before, more completely absurd, I muttered, "Oh, fuck
it" as I hoisted the dress back up over my head, letting it knock
the hat to the floor. I picked both up and draped them quickly
over a bed, pulled down the nylons (15 seconds, tops) and got
back into my shorts, my shirt, and my shoes meant for walking
in, and promptly and without any eye contact, left the room.

Outside I could think of nothing but to walk. Free of the
script for the first time in three days and free of the people in
uniforms monitoring my every move, I wasn't quite sure what I
might do. So I just walked around. I knew the time set for getting
the bride dressed, and I didn't have any intention of disappoint-
ing her (but would she really notice if there were six instead of
seven?), so I didn't go far. Anyway, there aren't many places to go
on Nantucket if you don't have a checkbook for buying art or a
bicycle and fancy linen clothes.

Re-entry two hours later didn't garner much attention or dis-
approval. One bridesmaid brought me to a hallway where my
dress was now hanging, and said in a snooty, irritated tone, "I had
to iron it *all over* again." But other than that, everyone was so
excited to start getting Annie dressed that nobody commented on
my outburst or departure. I suppose it's no more surprising that
such an odd addition to the party disappear for a time than it is
that she shows up in the first place. The bride got dressed, though
I don't think I helped at all. One would have had to put up a very

assertive passive aggressive fight in order to get physical access to her once the swarming began, and I didn't have the motivation or the social skills to wage such a war. But Annie was happy, and Peter about fainted when he saw her, just as he was supposed to, and the men wore polka-dotted bow ties and it all went along as weddings do.

I don't know where they are now, Annie and Peter. Maybe Peter's learning to grow organic vegetable for a co-op, or maybe they've opened a scuba diving school on a remote island in the South Pacific. The last tale I heard told of Peter's obsession with sustainable living and their intention to move to the mountains. Whatever it is he's found, I hope very much they are as joyous as ever. And I hope they still believe, when they find new Mexican restaurants, that those are the best damn enchiladas they've ever had, and that they still convince everyone to try them while they holler out in excitement and order a round of margaritas for people they hardly know.

The Revelation

I was drinking pints of Guinness and talking with Bruce the bartender when I understood what I had to do. I left my friends in the pub and ran several blocks to the phone booth. It was late and very dark when I put my coins into the dimly-lit machine and asked the operator for help calling Minnesota.

"Hello?"

"Mom, it's me. I'm going to graduate school."

"What? Are you ok? Where are you?"

"I want you to know that I'm going to graduate school. I'm going to teach literature to college students."

"What time is it? Where are you?"

"Mom, I'm serious. I know for sure and it's so great!"

There was a long pause, and I wondered if my message had gotten lost on a satellite orbiting above the North Sea.

"But you hate school," came the eventual reply.

I thought about this fact, the first glitch in my new plan, and dismissed it with all the flair a drunken and highly dramatic twenty-one-year-old can muster, which is a lot.

"Nnnnnnot any more!" I hollered into the phone, into the night, and up to the gods.

As I shouted this, I felt it needed italics of some sort—I felt that screaming at my mother from a phone booth at midnight on the edge of the Tay of Fife wasn't enough. I tried to raise my free hand up in the air, as if waving down a seaplane or celebrating my Wimbledon championship, but my hand collided painfully with the wall of the phone booth and I had to give it up. So I jumped up and down instead.

As mothers usually do, my mom had good reason to be suspicious. For most of my childhood, I didn't mind going to school per se. I just minded the sitting still, focusing, listening, reading, and paying attention aspects of the educational process. As a kid, I loved lunch period and gym and recess and marching down the hallways in lines. I liked art when they stopped talking and let you do things. But my, those teachers could talk.

As elementary school and junior high wore on, they talked more and more and let us run around and be foolish less, which was developmentally inappropriate for me, I'd just like to say. I would be far more effective in my current profession were my work day punctuated regularly with kickball games and little cartons of chocolate milk. In the main, to ease the pain of sitting still and to avoid listening, I was forever snickering and making jokes for anyone who would pay attention, and I suppose mine was the standard class clown pathology.

In high school, things eased up a bit because we got to choose our classes as long as we stayed within some very broad parameters. I made use of this freedom by avoiding most of the classes that required significant cerebral effort and honed both my class clown skills and my bullshitting capabilities. I took gym eight times instead of the required single semester, and I took music classes and photography classes (both of which came more easily to me and therefore were enjoyable rather than taxing) and yearbook classes and how to run a television camera classes and study hall, during which we simply left the building and did something else.

But the shit hit the fan in college. I applied my usual strategies to my new environment as best as I could. I enrolled in as many one-credit physical education classes as my schedule would allow and wondered why everybody wasn't banging down the doors to take Tumbling II, weight lifting, and beginning racquetball. And I tried to find an outlet for my jokester schtick.

In general, however, there was no getting around the serious business of academics in college. There was still room for jokes in this new environment, but the students telling them based their humor on the ideas being examined in the classes. They actually knew what they were talking about, which excluded me almost completely from the ranks of the funny. The classes were so very long and there were so few opportunities for being ridiculous that there seemed, finally, no other option but to sit down and discover what this paying attention business was all about.

So, a month or two into the first semester, I sat still and listened for the first time in my life. What I heard was mighty strange, and I concluded at first that the professors must have meant to be talking to somebody else, that they'd each walked into the wrong room or something. Once it became clear they were in the right place, I surmised the real problem. My college teachers seemed to harbor the grossly mistaken belief that I had paid attention to teachers sometime in my previous life, that I knew what a thesis was, could identify a pluperfect verb if my life depended on it, that I'd read *The Scarlett Letter* and the "Gettysburg Address," that I understood and cared how magnets worked, and knew how, when, and where to sit down, sit still, and accomplish an unreasonable amount of work.

I became an English major by default, and for the first year or so, I really tried to read the assignments in all of my classes. That got so frustrating so fast, however, that I eventually let it go. It was difficult to find the time to read things, and I wasn't learning much about time management, partly because I was so busy learning a lot about cheap beer management. And when I did complete a reading assignment, I'd generally be about as confused as you might expect a person who'd never really bothered to read before to be. I didn't know what we were reading the thing *for*. And I didn't know who was talking, in response to what, or to whom or why, and these are some really important questions.

Class was the last place I could expect to get answers to questions such as these, because my professors spoke as if we somehow already knew them and were now free to ponder the great significance of Arthur Millers' stage directions, or of rhyme and meter in Shakespeare's sonnets. And most of the other students sitting in the rooms with me seemed to think all of it made perfect sense, I suspect because they had been paying attention all along.

It was an American Novel class in particular that tipped the scales for me and sent me backwards from the ranks of the making-an-efforts to the already-given-ups. I read the first few novels we were asked to read, and I even liked them. Writers like Faulkner and Twain can tell a mighty fine story, after all. So I'd be excited to come to class, hoping to find kinship in my enjoyment of the book.

But in class this old mean guy would stand there and bellow at us, teaching us by way of intimidation by offering at every turn the opportunity for humiliation. He'd ramble on in complete incoherency about something we were supposed to already know and then dart out a question directed to a surprised student addressed by last name only. He was so full of "of course's" and "clearly's" and "as you know's" and not at all full of "let me explains" or "let's start at the beginning's" or "this man was a writer concerned about the nature of god and some people think he is important because's". Then would come the drilling questions, which he'd use as a transition to a new place in the text.

"Hemingway, of course, had a very strong reaction to the Spanish conflict, as you know ... Peabody! Tell us the significance of the metaphor on the bottom of page 161!"

Since his questions were so far out of my reach, it made no difference whether I'd read the material or not. My mind would go blank with worry every time he did it.

Thus began the grumpy "what's the use" phase of my thus-far non-stellar academic career. I'd tried, for godsake, on and off for months, and even that didn't help, so screw it.

I began again to rely on acting skills to save face in the class-room and on pure desperation to get by on exams and papers. The best way to avoid getting called on by a vindictive teacher is to pretend to be highly engaged in serious thought and to be writ-ing it down furiously, furrowed brows indicating your level of intense focus. Teachers don't pick on these people very often, opt-ing instead for those without the foresight to look busy.

If I did get called on—I had only a few options for reply. I could fumble through a less-than-complete answer by repeating something the teacher had said only moments before, using a tone that suggested I was just now wrapping my mind around the idea and wow, it's really fascinating. This gave him the satisfaction of thinking himself an effective teacher, which calmed his aggressive-ness. It also primed the tongues of those students who actually did know the answers and were then frustrated with my lame attempt, and so were prompted to jump in, cut me off, and offer a legitimate response to the question, thereby relieving me of my responsibility.

I could utter the powerful phrase, "I don't know. I've not thought about it in that way before," which, though honest, was an option to be used sparingly. And I could also—I was remark-ably good at this—parrot back a phrase I'd heard other students use while talking about the work before the teacher came in (I always arrived early to glean any such bits of information). Even though I usually only had a phrase and a vague idea of what part of the work it applied to, I could offer it and then cough irretriev-ably, giving only enough to indicate I had an interesting and rel-evant idea but could not articulate it just at that very moment.

Before one class on *Moby Dick* (there was no way in hell I was reading that monster just to be yelled at and further confused in class) I heard some overly hip and well-read students talking about the reading. I didn't know what they were talking about specifically, but I heard perfectly well when one of them shrugged off another's point and said dismissively, "it's just like Darwin. Survival of the fittest."

I walked to my seat and was handed a quiz asking a handful of plot-level questions about the reading. Such quizzes were standard, and I rarely knew the answers. Instead of writing the numbers one through five down the left margin of my paper, I wrote the simple sentence, "I don't remember, but the Darwinian themes were powerful." I got a C. I got a lot of C's in this manner, I suppose because the teachers assumed I wasn't as completely ignorant as I was and believed they saw sparks of something substantial. Or it could have been the case that when a person pays that many thousands of dollars to go to school, a C is about as bad as it gets if you show up and look like you're trying.

The best thing I ever did in college was leave. During my junior year, a friend mentioned that since our school was so grossly expensive, we could instead enroll in just about any university around the world, pay for airfare, transfer our credits, and still save our parents money. My parents were pretty busy remortgaging their house and selling their organs in order to make tuition payments so I could attend this college I'd chosen and been adamant about on the basis of no substantial information whatsoever, so I felt somewhat responsible for getting the most bang for their buck. Not responsible enough to complete all of the readings, you understand, but responsible enough to travel globally. Upon learning this was an option, I stopped my hacky sack game and walked immediately to the study abroad office.

Choosing quickly and of course randomly, I enrolled in a program for the fall of my senior year that would take me to a small-ish city in Scotland. I chose the place because I had never heard of it before, because it was way up high on the edge of Scotland which seemed cool, because it was an industrial town instead of a pretentious tourist town and I had had enough of pretension, and because why the hell not.

The only thing I know for certain about that part of Scotland, is that in 1988, a lot of students at the university there were extraordinarily drunk a great percentage of the time. I know because I was one of them and I had a lot of company. You could plunk me down in the middle of the city today and I would have no idea where I was. I don't remember the scenery, because life for me during those three months existed in two places: in pubs and in my head, the first making the second possible.

First, about the pubs. My drinking became more intense while I was abroad, as I guess it does for a lot of college travelers with the same unimpressive level of maturity I had. I had for three years participated happily in the see-how-much-you-can-drink culture at my own college, and what I had seen with no small amount of pride, was that I could drink an awful lot. But in Scotland I decided to push the experiment further, I suppose for a number of reasons. For one thing, the beer was just so damned good. To jump from Miller Lite out of kegs to Guinness out of a tap in a pub that knows just how cold to keep it, well, that's a coming-of-age story in itself.

On one holiday weekend, some friends and I drove west and caught a cheap flight to Dublin. On this trip I visited a pub on James Street in Dublin, just doors away from the famous Guinness brewery. Given my location, I ordered the only fashionable thing one could order, and was soon handed a beer that resembled a root beer float more than it did a Michelob.

I don't know whether it was the first Guinness I ever had, but I do know that it was the first Guinness I ever really understood. As I tipped my head back, my eyes closed and the room went silent. It was as if my brain understood that in order to appreciate what I was tasting at the moment, it had to shut down the rest of my senses, and this was fine with me. I drank the whole pint at once, never coming up for air because why would I, and I gestured to the bartender for another one, hoping he'd have it there before I was done with the first. He did. They're good at that, bartenders.

And on top of my discovery of great beer was the titillation I felt living in a culture that was so much more overt about its drinking habits. The building that served as the university's student union housed within its walls the standard amenities such as vending machines, a swimming pool, a weight room, lockers, and information desks. But it also housed no fewer than five pubs. On any given night there would be boisterous men belting out Scottish folk tunes to live bagpipes in one, serious dart tournaments in another, rock music in another, and students reading books while quietly nursing their pints in still another.

I rather liked this up-front nature of the university's approach to belly wash consumption. Instead of making students arrange for their own kegs in dorm rooms or travel off campus, they just built drinking into student life. Had a tough class? Have a pint. Anxious about your grades? Have an ale. Just woke up? Of course you did, have a stout. Forget you're supposed to be taking classes. No worries. Have another and join us for a dart match, won't you?

And so I joined the legions of other students at the University who pretty much started drinking when they got up and stopped only when they fell down from exhaustion.

Miraculously, this excessive activity did not curtail my involvement in other activities. I went to aerobics regularly, though every now and then I fell over while attempting very simple movements. And of course I went to classes. I know very well that it's highly irritating to be around drunks. I also know that it's far less irritating to actually be a drunk, at least while the fun lasts.

And what's really cool is that instead of leading to alcoholism, which it could have, or to an ill-advised midnight leap into the Tay, which it could have, or to a loss of brain function or other serious illness, which it should have, my drinking led me directly to a new and many times richer intellectual life.

As a highly emotional, ultra-empathizer who is always aware of how other people are feeling about all sorts of things, including me, the self confidence and social freedom that came with drunkenness provided a welcome sense of isolation and relief. Sure, I was several thousand miles away from anything familiar, and that helped a great deal. But I traveled much farther by leaving my sobriety behind. Sometimes one's inhibitions can be stifling, after all.

So onto the cerebral part. I had two English classes, both of which were necessary for my college graduation only months away. One of these classes was on Scottish authors. This class met in the lecturer's office, as there were only six or seven of us and he had comfortable chairs. At the beginning of class, he'd hand around a tray of snifters, which was followed by brandy or cognac. Once we were all loosened up and he began to feel chatty—sometimes five minutes into class, sometimes thirty—he'd clear his throat, offer a personal compliment to the drink we were enjoying, and crack open a book. He'd summon from deep within him Robert Burns himself and read to us of unending love: "And I will luve thee still, my dear, while the sands o life shall run." He'd read to us shamelessly of glory, and of loss, of pride in haggis, and of fear of wrath at home. And he'd read with such love for the stuff that we loved it too. We all did. He brought several of us to tears regularly, and after class I would walk to the pub feeling like Robert Burns and John Galt were walking right there with me.

Now this was an interesting phenomenon. My cavalier attitude toward the class was born of the assumption that since little outside work was required and there were few tests or papers and since we were drinking in class, I was getting away with something. In the meantime, I was hearing and enjoying literature for just about the first time in my life. Our teacher didn't ask that we respond to it from a feminist or formalist or any other perspective. He didn't take it apart or hold it up to be anything it wasn't. And perhaps most importantly, he didn't hold himself up to be anything more than he was. He was just a guy who wanted us to hear this stuff that he loved. And hear it we did.

My other English class was called the Twentieth Century British Novel, and this is where the earth really started to shift beneath my feet. In this class the lecturer came into our room on the first day without a syllabus. Instead, she presented us with a list of all of the twentieth-century British novelists she knew of. We had the hour, she said, to ask questions about these authors, which she'd do her best to answer. At the end of the class, she continued, we would vote on the three authors we wished to study in the course.

So we asked questions. We asked who these authors were. We asked which ones were popular and why, and we asked which ones were studied most often and why. We asked which ones were doing something new, and we asked which ones told the best love stories. We asked which were short, which were dense, which our instructor loved and why. We asked which ones she knew the least about. We asked all sorts of things; no questions were out of bounds. Can you imagine? We started a learning experience at the beginning. It was shocking.

For our second class, the teacher gave us lists of the novels written by the authors we'd chosen, and we followed a similar process to select which of those books we'd study. We had our questions ready: Are any of them funny? Which ones deal with what it's like being on your own for the first time? Did he fight in the war? Why was she so worried about upper class manners, and why should we care? Why do critics pay so much attention to this one but not that one?

I had assumed at the beginning of this process that we'd try to ferret out which books would be the easiest and therefore the most fun, but as she stood there and answered our questions as fully and honestly as she was able to, we became more and more interested in tackling authors considered by others in the field to be complex or important or interesting. Once the formulaic romance or suspense writers were identified, for example, few students showed further interest in them. If she was going to let us start at the beginning, that meant we had the freedom to pursue tougher questions without fear of not having known the answers already, and I was not alone in responding enthusiastically. It was as if we'd suddenly been given permission to join an elite club. And with the door hanging open like that, few in the room seemed inclined to continue pretending we hadn't wanted in all along.

At the end of the second class period, the instructor passed around a sheet of paper listing all of the novels up for grabs and wrote a one-sentence assignment on the board: "write your name next to the novel of your choosing, and begin your preparations for teaching that novel to the rest of us." She didn't say much at all about how we should "teach" the classes we were signing up to teach. She just told us to find the books in bookstores and get to work.

It doesn't matter which title I signed up for. It only matters that I did, that I went back to my room and read it, that I liked it, that I had questions about it that even my peers and instructor thought were important and worth pursuing, that I read it again and then read four other books by the same author, that I began to use research to learn things, and that I loved it.

The night after my class had its first discussion of the novel I'd prepared to teach, I sat in a pub with my friends. Instead of keeping track of the cricket score, my head was full of Robert Burns, this dead man with whom I shared both nothing and everything in common. And it was filled with a hundred questions from that day's discussion of a novel, a discussion that took place with me, of all unlikely candidates, at the front of the room. There I was, leading, redirecting, pressing for more, questioning. I left the pub and raced to a phone booth to call home and announce my newly discovered career path. I've never looked back.

When my college gave me a largely unmerited Bachelor's degree a few months later, I knew I had years of work to catch up on. Before I could entertain the thought of graduate school I had to take the time to read all the books I'd ignored and reread those

I'd refused to engage with. I had to retake classes, and to learn how to write a paper and to do all sorts of other things a normal college graduate should already know how to do. And my beer consumption slowed substantially when there was no more room for it on my credit card and I found myself responsible for mundane expenses such as rent and groceries. So my leap to graduate school was neither immediate nor without its own set of humiliations and surprises. Nevertheless, it was a leap that changed everything.

Now I teach English at a community college, and my students and I have a fine time peering into the academic world in which none of us has ever felt entirely at home. My knowledge of what it's like on the outside helps me open doors for students fumbling around out there just like I did, and sometimes I can do this with humor, cracking well-deserved jokes at academia to help loosen the hinges. Underneath the jokes, though, my teaching is driven by two things. I confront the earliest signs of bullshit with a tenacity my students find overdone, and I always—always—start at the beginning.

That's Only
If It's Just You

Just after college, I had a joyous time not having any idea what I was doing. The whole world was like gym class then, and I was free to eat all the candy I wanted. I had faith, finally, that someday I would be a serious person teaching literature and so had no anxiety about my future in that regard; and there is nothing quite so fun as putting seriousness off for a few more years. We should all do it a lot more often.

With one semester of college remaining and more than a year of make-up reading to do before I could entertain graduate school applications, I hatched a plan that seemed simple enough. I'd pick a new city to live in, get the job I had earned, read some actual books, and be as foolish as all get out.

My college friend Christine, a woman who matches my preferred level of sustained ridiculousness at every turn, came from a small town in Massachusetts. Hers is the kind of town where kids buy houses a few doors down from their parents, and so on, until several generations and multiple branches of the same family can be bitten by the same mosquito.

Her departure for a college as far away as upstate New York had already caused enough ruckus in the family, and her post-graduation plans were to return to her hometown and look for

70

work, mostly because it hadn't occurred to her to do anything else. Thrilled to learn there was another option, when she heard my pick-a-city scheme, she jumped aboard, and, happily, our destinies were sealed together.

The matter of which city to pick and live in was resolved in a single night with a cover story, an atlas, and a lot of beer. In a random magazine we found a list of the ten best cities to live in, based on whose standards we had no idea—they could have been the best cities for small dog owners, or for people living in nursing homes. Not caring a whit where the list came from, we located these cities on the atlas, considered our desire to go far away from where we were sitting at the time, recalled a hazy stereotype of Seattle as a lefty kind of town, and made our decision. Christine's parents responded as if we'd announced we were moving to Minsk. They got out a globe to show her younger siblings where she was going, and once we got there and she called home, they hung up immediately, assuming the phone call would cost something in the neighborhood of one hundred and eighty-seven dollars.

Anyway, we planned carefully. We would work all summer, so as to amass the fortunes we'd need for the move, and then we'd head out in the fall. I worked at a summer camp leading backpack trips and teaching girls how to saddle horses, Christine worked in a popsicle factory, and we saved money like only highly delusional young people can while facing a major and grossly expensive life change. I picked up Christine in New York State in August, and the two of us drove across highway 90 pulling a U-Haul trailer behind a loaded Toyota Tercel hatchback. The car sputtered and whined at 30 miles per hour over the Rockies. We paid no mind and carried on, belting out "Blame it on the Rain" by the soon-to-be disgraced, Milli Vanilli (they were robbed, by the way. Pop music isn't supposed to be authentic). After paying for gas and food along the way and a few truck-stop showers, I had five hundred dollars to my name, and my friend had about three hundred.

When we arrived in Seattle it was a Sunday morning, and we sat in a little upscale bakery looking at the newspaper and drinking tea, figuring for unknown reasons that tea was the most appropriate beverage for soon-to-be upper middle class, young professionals in Seattle. We ordered large cups of tea because we had some significant things to accomplish. We planned to find an apartment and some jobs, and so head off by noon to get started with our adult lives. We did find an apartment we could move into right away, though it was far seedier and demanded more of our cash than anything either of us had imagined. We signed a lease that day at the Totem apartments, which were created when somebody took a cheap and moldy old motel, linked a few rooms together here and there, and glued efficiency kitchenettes onto some walls. I don't know if the totem pole out front that provided our apartment's theme was there when the place was a motel or if the guy who took two or three weeks to turn it into an apartment complex thought of it. The "gold chenille couch cover" promised in the newspaper ad was a nasty smelling rag, and the "aqua arm chairs" beside it were plastic, but, having exactly no other choice, we moved right in and called it home. We did not, however, find the jobs we expected to—not that morning anyway, or any morning after that, though our spirits remained high.

After years of hearing about the economic disadvantages of not having a college degree, we quite naturally assumed that having a college degree would translate into tangible advantages. Our humble assumption was that we would have our pick of jobs if we were willing to settle for thirty or forty grand a year, a modest concession required by our being fresh out of school and not having skills, experiences, or any presentable clothes.

Unable to locate any of these jobs in the paper that morning, we did see some other interesting listings. The most hopeful ad in the paper promised "$100 a night just for serving drinks!" After forking over nearly all of our cash to our new landlord, we had about $80 left, and by the next day, a crisp Monday morning, we were a bit more realistic about our job expectations. We somberly admitted that it would probably take time to find our professional jobs—maybe a week or more—and that ensuing paychecks would be still weeks behind that. So we pursued work that could sustain us in the meantime. We called the number in the paper; we landed interviews for that very same afternoon. We went out to lunch ($25) to celebrate our good fortune.

Arriving at the address given to us over the phone, we were surprised to find, right there in the middle of gloriously organic, yogafied, alternative press-leaning Seattle, a wood-paneled trailer home. Inside the shaggy-carpet, living room-turned-lobby, a woman who I was sure would make a great prostitute sat at a receptionist's desk and chatted with us in a tone that was odd because it assumed the air of a we're-all-in-this-together kind of commiseration. She stood up on grotesquely high heels and leaned forward, using the Dolly Parton balancing technique of thrusting her bottom back and her chest forward, and then gently squished our hands with the tips of her fingers in a mock handshake, as if we weren't the sort of people to really shake hands but should nevertheless follow through with the general idea of that script. "This your first time working for Rick?" she asked, sitting back down and chomping loudly on her gum. After alerting her boss to our presence by way of a yell over her shoulder, she sat behind her desk and stared vacantly out the window. There were no papers or office supplies on her desk, no way to tell that she did anything there at all. "He's alright. I seen a lot worse," she said, welcoming us into the fold with sisterly warmth. I wasn't sure what standard she was using for comparison, and did not bond with the receptionist. I only wondered how she could be so stupid as to sit there making probably minimum wage when she could be making "$100 a night just for serving drinks!"

Once inside the actual office, our real-world expectations took their first significant hits. Christine had been called in first, and ten minutes later Rick came out an invited me to join them. When

I came into the room I tried to make meaningful eye contact with my friend, to ascertain whether we would or would not get the jobs, whether it was good news or bad. But she just stared past me from her chair across the bedroom-turned-office with a strange smile pulling across her face, as if someone else had put it there and, though it was painful, she had no power to remove it.

Rick had a dark, greasy comb-over, he wore a silvery, disco-patterned shirt unbuttoned nearly to his navel, and he leaned back in his old swivel chair with his cowboy boots propped on a desk, on which sat, no kidding, a half-empty bottle of Jack Daniels. I couldn't think of a single thing to add to the scene that would make him any more of a cliché, but I kept my focus on the much-needed $100. He stretched his arms behind his head and smiled warmly as he greeted me, focusing intently on my ass and chest. I don't think he ever met my eye. I kept looking at Christine for some indication of what was going on, but she wouldn't meet my eye either.

He did offer us jobs serving drinks, and he did promise we'd make a minimum of $100 a night, just like the ad said. We were given the address of the club, driving instructions so specific even my cat could follow them, and our breasts were given another warm smile, the kind of attention my breasts, at least, had not gotten ever before and have not gotten since. Then, in a tone that suggested he was wrapping things up, he happened to mention that since we weren't dancing, "at least for now," we could wear miniskirts and tank tops, as long as they were fairly tight.

"Excuse me, I'm sorry … *what?*" I stammered, as my friend sat rigidly in her chair, pained smile still frozen in place.

"Oh the dancing," he nodded, knowingly, waving the trifling problem out of the air with a dismissive flip of his hand. "Yeah, it's topless. You don't have any problem with that, do you?"

When neither of us could think of a single thing to say in response this question, he commenced to sooth the feathers he sensed, rightly, to be shockingly ruffled. "A lot of girls come in here, they think the dancing's going to be a big deal, but you know what? I bet you *money* ... " and at this he leaned forward and thumped his pointer finger on the desk, " ... that once you see what kind of cash those girls make when they are dancing, you'll be right back here and you'll be *begging* me to dance—I give it two weeks."

Then his eyes turned from us to face the window, and for an awkward, silent moment, he acted as a man deep in thought. We sat in stunned silence until he turned back quickly and with a look of excitement on his face. "Hey!" he said loudly, addressing Christine's midsection, "I bet you're Italian, right?"

Though not the most clever young women ever to graduate from college and head into the world, we were astute enough not to believe him when he launched into the shtick designed to help us understand first that our destiny was in topless dancing, and second that the only reason we were wary of accepting our fate was that we grossly misunderstood the reality of the situation. Now he spoke in warm, reassuring tones, as if he were our father cooing at us after a nightmare and promising that everything will be OK because Daddy is here.

"I know it seems like a big deal now, dancin' topless. I'd feel the same way if I were you. I swear to *god* I would ..."

At least he understands the problem, I thought.

"But the thing is, you see, *that's* only if it's just you up on that stage. But you get twenty, thirty girls up there at the same time, and you'll never know the difference. I'll put you two on as waitresses, but you'll want to be dancing real soon. Wait'll you see."

We didn't wait to see, but we did get in the car and laugh until our lungs threatened to seize up, and we did race to a pay phone to call home and announce we'd gotten our first, post-college job offers. Once our respective parents understood the situation, we each held up the receiver so that the other could hear the identical responses screaming over the phone wires first from Minnesota and minutes later from Massachusetts: "*You come home right now!*"

Back at the Totem, Christine and I had a meeting to discuss our situation. We counted our remaining dollars and considered all that had happened since we'd arrived in Seattle. It was quickly established that we were having a marvelous time and that we should therefore celebrate. First, though, we figured we should look more seriously toward the future and do some long-term planning. So we signed and mailed an expensive monthly contract for membership in a health club that was miles away from the Totem, figuring we should get this task out of the way because who wants to be shopping for a health club while getting used to a new job, and not figuring anything about the forty mile drive or the monthly fees at all. We made a budget, though one that rested on the hypothetical jobs and accompanying paychecks we assumed were speeding their way into our lives. And we agreed that restaurant celebrations would henceforth be limited to one per day and to all-you-can-eat buffets that accepted VISA, raising a minor problem that was quickly solved with our promise to pay off said credit cards with our first real paychecks. Finally, to demonstrate that we were now officially grown up, we went to a grocery store instead of a restaurant and charged the food and drink necessary to celebrate.

After that, Christine and I worked at several different jobs and failed to get many others. There were more assembly lines and more strange temporary assignments, and there were a lot of rejections from outfits looking to fill professional positions. I did get one other job offer that I turned down, which, like the topless job, paid decently. It would have meant working for an animal rescue operation, which was fine, but what they needed was someone to euthanize twenty to forty abandoned pets per day. Surely there are more enticing ways to lure young people toward a particular career path. And I even got an open, unapologetic scoff from a "professional headhunter" who felt no need to hide her amusement at my complete lack of qualifications for any work she'd ever heard of. It took months, though, for any of this to sink in.

For much of the fall I worked at a restaurant and bar serving drinks with my clothes on, while keeping my eye on the Sunday paper's classified section and waiting for my increasingly illusive job to appear. I worked the breakfast shift at first, but found it to be such a bother that I limited my time to the night shifts. Breakfast work was grueling, and breakfast eaters were both unappreciative and stingy. The nighttime patrons were extraordinarily drunk undergraduate students and people looking to sleep with extraordinarily drunk undergraduate students. Their credit cards were even shinier than mine, and their driver's licenses were so obviously fake that I was always tempted to ask what mean dental instrument they'd used to alter their birthdates.

With the right attitude, serving drinks to drunk people was far more enjoyable than serving food to sober people. It was certainly a lot more lucrative, and the patrons were always so damned happy. Drunken frat boys could be easily overcharged or convinced to tip heavily and repetitively if they were trying to impress, as was always the case, either each other or equally drunk females. At night, the place was downright nasty, but neither the forever-chanting and chest-thumping young men nor the scantily-clad, nearly passed out young women draped over chair backs seemed to mind. The tables could be coated in sixteen layers of dried beer and sex on the beaches, they could have two partially-eaten French fries and a chunk of someone's green-apple lip gloss literally stuck in place, and the customers couldn't have been any more pleased with their environment or those of us there to serve them. "Saraaaa!" They'd holler. Many would put their arms around me and introduce me to their equally-smashed friends: "Shara's my bud. Hey dude! Shara here is my good friend and if you want anything, just ask cause she's awesome. Say Rah! Say Rah! Dude, I gotta pee, maybe puke, I dunno." Being an extrovert, I really appreciated the fact that the people I was stealing from liked me.

By Christmas, I understood that I was not going to find my professional job paying thirty or forty thousand dollars a year—

there would be no impressive title, no company vision or mission statement to brag about, no desk, no salary, no stapler, no multi-line phone. Other than the chance to kill puppies and kittens by the dozen, I never found a single job that was made available to me on the basis of my college degree, and I consider this fact in silence when I urge my current students to move beyond our community college and finish up at a four-year institution. So, giving up the job search, I settled, finally, into a position that offered the next best thing, which was the opportunity to be surrounded by the office supplies appropriate to the nondescript professional work I thought I wanted. With Christine's help, I got a job working at a copy store where she was already a lead shift worker, being the only shift worker. Our primary responsibilities were to help people make copies for six cents apiece, send their faxes, and play with office equipment of every variety.

Not having professional jobs, we decided, once again, not to behave as professional people. We made copies of most of our body parts and faxed them late at night to our college administrative offices. We blew up the cover of Prince's Lovesexy album and faxed that to people we knew and people we didn't know. We made reams of personal letterhead, Christmas cards, posters advertising non-events, and various presents for friends. We drank an entire five gallon jug of water in an eight-hour shift simply to see if it was possible, and generally looked for and discovered entertainment everywhere in the store. When the newspaper reported that a local fraternity was busted forcing its recruits to do awful things with sheep and peanut butter, we kept up on the scandal by reading the faxes they asked us to send to their national headquarters. In their faxes the disgraced young men begged for forgiveness and swore over and over again that the sheep were only at the frat house to participate in a skit about the dangers of hazing. Life is hilarious if you just look at it in the right way.

That we often didn't have enough food was a problem that required some attention, but even that didn't merit our unhappiness. We celebrated the chance to live on refried bean burritos for months at a time, and we were happy to share apples during our work breaks. We enjoyed getting to know the sample ladies at the local grocery store, and we met new friends while patronizing happy hours with buffets, buying a single cheap beer and stuffing our pockets with chicken wings and chips. Once, we waited in line at a shelter for food, but went home before we got to the front, unsure whether what we were doing was appropriate. And early in the year, Christine had the last $50 she owned stolen from her by a jogging thief as she stood downtown in front of an ATM machine. Instead of going out to celebrate my birthday like she'd planned, we stayed at the Totem, ate cheap cupcakes and drank more beer, and considered ourselves lucky to be able to have such a fabulous time.

At the end of the year Christine stayed in Seattle to pursue, well, the rest of her life, and I headed east in search of mine, bidding my dear friend farewell and closing the door on the most joyously foolish year of my life. We'd been idiots all year, and we didn't care enough to stop laughing, not ever. Without enough money to foresee paying the rent every month, without good jobs, and generally without any but the most moronic of plans, we discovered the company of a good friend and the joy of living were enough. Now I have the professional job I could never find in Seattle; I have a lot of good friends, and I can afford groceries. And somehow, I get smothered easily with fears that my expectations might be too high, that the world will somehow disappoint me, or, worse, that I'll disappoint myself. But when I think back on Seattle, I know that it would be far better for all of us if every few years we could put off being serious for a few more years. I know better than to stop finding reasons to laugh.

Part II

Pretty Damn
Clever, If You Ask Me

I've spent a great deal of time in the first 40 years of my life trying to understand the lure of the Republican Party. For years I've been trying to figure out why they, of all people, happen to have been in charge for so long at this particular juncture in human history. And they're a hard bunch to get a handle on. One minute they're busy doing the right thing and going to war to abolish slavery and the next thing you know they are even busier going to war somewhere else in order to distract us from their efforts at home, which seem clear enough when I read beyond the front page of the paper: Here they are working feverishly to abolish public spaces, to abolish public retirement funds, to abolish public assistance, and to abolish public access to fine health care, education, clean water, clean air, and a free media system.

They're big on abolition; that I can see. What I can't see, though, is anybody still votes for these guys. And we didn't just elect them. We elected them, suffered the consequences, and then rushed to our local schools, churches and community centers—at least the ones lucky enough to have enough voting machines—to re-elect them.

Since I was raised in a political bubble and knew well not a single Republican, my journey to understand conservatives had to begin, out of sheer necessity, at the beginning. And so I stepped out of my bubble. At my small but grossly expensive college in upstate New York, I met conservatives for the first time, and so began to unravel the mystery at hand.

Our first semester in college, we all had to take a Liberal Arts class, part of which included a small discussion group of about twenty students and one professor. The class examined a wide range of readings on the human condition. I can't be more specific because I didn't actually complete many of the reading assignments, but the general drift of the conversation was clear enough.

In this discussion group, I came to understand pretty quickly the make-up of one type of conservative. The most outspoken students in my class were conservatives, and they also happened to be mighty rich. They were heirs, for godsake, and they played polo. Among these students on campus were the sons and daughters of major advertising, law, design, and brokerage executives or of foreign ambassadors and in one case the dignitary of a tyrannical foreign government.

I suppose we're all heirs of one sort or another. I've already inherited my grandmother's hips and a sleeping disorder that makes it hard for me to avoid kicking my partner repeatedly at night. But you don't go around introducing yourself as an heir where I come from, and you don't house ponies in stables or anywhere else, unless of course you run a pony ride. It isn't done.

During the first meeting of the discussion group, our professor asked us to introduce ourselves, and while doing so, to say a little something about our goals over the next four years. I mumbled my name and stammered through a few lines about taking some neat classes and maybe joining the swim team. The tall guy sitting to my right looked down on me with disdain, and then stuck his chest out and boomed. "I am Arthur Philip Sexton the Third, and my intention is to get the degree I'll need to make a hell of a lot of money." This is the same guy who later, during a discussion about ethics, offered the following sage advice: "What matters is to make money. You step on whoever you need to step on, and you step as hard as you have to."

And so I learned lesson number one. For people like this, being a conservative means believing that money should be conserved in one's very own pockets—unless, if I understand correctly, it's in somebody else's pocket, in which case that person should be stepped on and her money taken, so that it resides, finally, in the stepper's pocket, where it is to be forever conserved.

While the hemorrhaging liberal that is me finds this a troublesome credo for life, it is nevertheless an easy one to understand. I like conserving what I have too, after all, and even though what I have isn't massive wealth, I can still mostly understand the principle. For example, at lunchtime I'm going to enjoy the last of a batch of enchiladas my partner made, and if anybody should swoop in and take said enchiladas before I get to them, I'll be really mad. And sometimes, when we're at dinner, I'm not happy with just one helping of lasagna, and I eye my son's portion, hoping he'll look the other way so I can sneak a bite from his plate. Now I'm pretty sure I'd never step on him, hard or otherwise, to get Italian food, but we're all different.

However, while it makes sense that some rich people want to remain rich people and become even richer, this does little to explain the elections and re-elections of people like Ronald Reagan and George W. Bush.

In 1984, Fifty-four million Americans voted for Reagan's second round of shenanigans. And in 2004, sixty-two million people voted to re-elect Bush. Now I know that it takes more than one to play a sound polo match and that my hyper-rich college peers had families, friends, and other connections to more people as rich as they were—that there are entire clubs, schools, neighborhoods and shops full of these people and nobody else—but I am also savvy enough to know that there are not fifty-four or sixty-two million people in this country who entertain the hope of ever participating in a polo match. I bet there aren't even that many people in this country who know somebody who knows somebody who plays polo, assuming Prince Charles doesn't count, which I fully do.

So who votes for these guys? Bush wasn't elected by people wanting to conserve money. He was funded by them, sure, but that's just not the whole story. To grossly oversimplify without losing accuracy, he was taking money away from rather than giving it to too many people for that to be the case. I think that in order to answer this question we have to be willing to apply the word "conserve" to all sorts of things, excepting, of course, public air, water, assistance, privacy, education, health care, parks, and other minor quality-of-life considerations.

A few years after college I so effectively irritated the English Department at the University of Tennessee that they relented and said I could come and try my luck as a graduate student. After I packed up my car and prepared to move, I noted in my atlas that Tennessee was in the southern half of the United States. It's a long and skinny state tucked down there among states like Kentucky, Georgia, Mississippi, and Alabama, the states that always land so many starring roles in Hollywood Civil Rights movies that I've come to believe they must have an inside connection to Steven Spielberg or Ron Howard because nobody gets that lucky that often in auditions.

In the south I met a very different kind of conservative, and it was here that I began to understand why at least some non-super-rich people might like Reagan and Bush, not to mention Fred Thompson, Bill Frist, and Van Hilleary.

It's not about the money there. Arthur Philip Sexton the Third would be run out of town with pelt marks from spit chew on his backside were he ever to introduce himself the way he did in my Liberal Arts class in college. In Knoxville, Tennessee, gross amounts of cash are not heaped up in the same person's pockets very often, unless you're a lawyer or a coach for the

University's football team—and even then, we're still not talking international ambassadorships and collections of Vercace handbags.

While I was in Tennessee, political ads worked the same way they do everywhere else—by creating their audience's fears and then appealing to those fears by promising to make everything right again, you know, the way it was before the commercial started. In my favorite political ad of the 1990s, shown on television in Tennessee, the candidate stood on the porch of a house out in the country, a house surrounded, of course, by a white picket fence. As the ad opened he was looking off into the fields, tensely awaiting some unknown newcomer, his arms crossed defiantly over his chest. Dramatic music told us all to feel afraid, and to notice how brave this guy was to stand up to whatever or whoever was coming down the road. Then the candidate turned his head so he faced the camera directly without moving the rest of his body, as if he was comforting his cowering wife and children as they hid behind the couch inside the house: "When I'm your Senator," he promised, "I'll keep the government out of your pocketbook and off your property." He never raised a sawed off shot gun, but one got the feeling it wasn't very far away.

For many people in the south (and in the north—that I discovered this in Tennessee does not limit the phenomenon geographically, though concentrations are, as they say, high), the conservative part of conservative politics means conserving some peculiar traditions, keeping things the way they were a long time ago, or at least the way some people wish they were a long time ago.

In the main, living in the south means living with the general belief that things have gone sour, and that if we could just get them back the way they were everything would be well again. This is a powerful belief system, and marketers and politicians seem to have figured this out. Southern tourist attractions bank on their reputation for this kind of nostalgia by offering no end of the Ye Olde Shoppes and Ye Olde Shacks selling images of a poverty-ridden but apparently happy southern life that exists not in history, but in commercial myth.

That these images are used to beckon us to get out of our cars and buy a plate of all-you-can-eat shrimp seems dreadfully ironic. I suppose they work the way all stereotypes work. They confirm our need not to feel guilty, and in the land of commercials, this freedom makes us much better shoppers. Want someone to buy something? Show him a picture of poor folk who don't have proper clothing and have not eaten enough lately but who are gratefully, fortunately, and obviously very happy. See the cute, simple, starving child? Ooh, I feel a powerful hunger coming on. Honey, pull over at that adorable little prefabricated shrimp shack, won't you?

There are probably more billboards on highways in the south featuring a small, freckled white boy in ripped and tattered overalls, an old straw hat and no shirt, fishing with a crooked branch for a fishing rod and smiling to show us he is missing several teeth than there ever were actual boys like this. And I wish someone would make a public service announcement to be aired during the Super Bowl and in all public and private schools educating every last one of us about the use of the damned Ye. The "Y" in "Ye" is a close relative to a middle English letter, the thorn, that we don't use anymore and that indicated a "th" sound. "Ye" was pronounced "the" all along, and so there never was a real Ye Olde anything anywhere, and Pigeon Forge, Tennessee wasn't around to have these ice cream shoppes in the Middle Ages anyway so what the hell?

Anyway, this second kind of conservative thinking means different things for different people. For many, apparently—as the television ad about the politician-turned-protector-of-porches ad worked—it means conserving a time before the government regularly trod upon front lawns, which is tough on the grass, and rifled through people's pockets—a sort of wild west, you-stake-it, you-claim-it era, when the livin' was hard but full of nostalgic and entirely imaginary glory. These conservative folks were delighted with the prospect of a Y2K disaster, and happily stored up generators, ammo, and cans of processed meats, looking forward to the day when they'd be able to guard their own porches in the same way they imagined their luckier ancestors once had. It doesn't matter that the Republican Party is no longer the party of small government. It matters only that they look and bluster accordingly.

So conservative politicians can appeal to all sorts of people hoping to conserve something, something other than public education, public parks, the arts, the middle class and all public … well, you get the point. And more popular than money or the wild west, however, is a mighty peculiar set of rules a great number of people in this country are turning to their politicians to help them conserve: a set of rules dictating how men and women ought and ought not behave. Really. This is a bigger-than-war, healthcare, crime, and poverty type deal for a lot of people. Way bigger.

For these folks, Bush wasn't popular because he was part of the oil industry or because of how much he was worth. He was popular because he's manly and the women in his family are very much not, and we need more of that 'round here by god. He had a ranch on which there was brush that needed a'clearin from time to time, and he had some flannel shirts. He liked to thump his chest and he liked to stick to his guns, more literally than is comfortable to say.

Just as important was how his wife behaved. In 2006, Laura Bush was in the news talking about her exercise routine. In the interview, the Missus responded to questions about her own workouts by repeatedly comparing them to the manlier workouts of her husband, about which nobody was asking. She needed a nonthreatening domestic issue to support, as all conservative first ladies must have, and hers was health and fitness. It is true that we're all getting really fat, and there is no question that health and fitness would be a good idea for Americans in general, but this is a tricky issue for a conservative woman to tackle, you see, because she must promote exercise while showing that she can stay in her womanly place. So in her interview, Laura Bush says she works out, but promises that the exercise isn't crossing any lines. She lifts weights, yes, but promises that they are only "3-to-5" pound weights, nothing like what George, who is "a natural athlete" lifts.

Now, what with being a happily-married-in-Canada lesbian, I have a hard time understanding why so many people want to conserve such models for human behavior. I guess that when I hear that a woman lifts weights, I'm OK with the idea that some of them might be heavier than your average butternut squash. And I don't mind men who like to read and are capable of complex thought, nuance, or depth. I guess I just like to mix things up a bit more than some folks do.

So I don't know *why* this is such a big deal to people, but I know that it is. Accordingly, conserve it they will, and as I discovered, this very popular form of conservatism has a way of yoking the rest of us into its harness whether we like it or not.

The great benefit of this form of conservatism is that it often comes, if you fit the part, with a level of civility that I've never seen anywhere else. In the south, I got so used to people helping me and holding open doors and calling me Honey and Darlin that I could barely function when first I moved back to the comparatively harsh level of civility required in day-to-day interactions in Minnesota.

It's nice to be treated nicely. I like it a lot. On one road trip from St. Paul to Knoxville I faced terrible weather for nearly the entire sixteen-hour drive. As I was increasingly tired, and as the rain kept pouring, I got lonely and craved real human interaction. At a gas station outside of Chicago, the clerk didn't even look up at me through the window that separated us, opting instead to shove my change back through the slot below while chatting on the phone with somebody else.

But much later that night I was in Kentucky, in no city or town at all, just stopped in the middle of farm and horse country at a self-serve gas station. My back was sore and my eyes were bloodshot and my body smelled of car. I doubt that I smiled as I pulled up, miserable as I was. But the guy working at the gas station, the only other person there, acted from the moment I parked under his brightly lit awning like I was his long lost niece, suddenly found in the middle of a thunderstorm.

He offered to pump my gas for me, sent me inside ahead of him, and told me where to find some coffee. He made me sit down on the chair behind the register and have a rest where it was warm. He showed me pictures of his dog, which was wearing some kind of blue bow on its head. He went outside again to check my tires, and while he was out there he checked my oil too. He checked my wiper blades. He made me promise that I was sure I could continue driving and would not fall asleep. He refused payment for anything but the gas, and stood out in the rain—no kidding—waving as I drove off into the dark night. He didn't know who I was and never asked. I was so grateful I cried.

But at other times, the kindness extended to me in the south seemed to have a whole lot less to do with helping me and a whole lot more to do with establishing the manly character of the person offering the kindness. When I was still new in town, I'd actually argue with boys in grocery and hardware stores over whether I was or was not going to carry my bag of apples and cheese or my single two-by-four to my own vehicle. Full of northern chutzpah, I felt a formidable feminist in a landscape that needed me.

But it wasn't long until I gave up. In a grocery store parking lot, fresh off of a successful attempt to carry out my own bags all by myself, a manager swept up beside me while I was walking and took the bags out of my hand without asking. He walked behind and to the side of me until I reached my pick-up truck, and as he slid my groceries across the front seat and held my door open for me to get in, he bade me "have a good night, ma'am" before shutting my door. You wouldn't think from looking at me that I had a lot of lady potential, but some of these men were determined that I know my place and allow them theirs. You can't have gentlemen without ladies, I suppose. They wouldn't have anything to do, what with dueling being so passé and the civil war being so over.

When I moved back to Minnesota, I needed sand bags to weigh down the rear wheels in my truck if it was going to get me through the snow. So I approached a cashier in a hardware super-store and paid for four of the seventy-pound bags I'd seen stacked up by the door on my way in. I'd lived in the south for eight years, and so when I handed the cashier my check, I asked where I should drive my truck to have the bags loaded for me.

She looked at me oddly, and then said, "Oh, sure. Let me see if there's someone at the service desk. Pull up to the front there."

So I followed directions and sat in my truck next to the stack of sand bags, waiting. I could think of nothing to say—noth-ing—when eventually a sixty year-old woman came out, barking, "You the one needs these bags?" She had one slung over her shoul-der and was moving briskly toward the back of my truck when she explained, "hell, you can do this, can't you? It's no different than lifting a kid."

I didn't have time to explain my stupidity. I just jumped up and grabbed a bag, easily thumping it in the truck as she dumped the last two behind it.

In many of the classrooms where I taught at the University of Tennessee, the chalk ledges at the bottom of the chalk boards were located thirty-five inches above the floor, a height that happens to correspond precisely with the middle of my butt. Since I stood and often leaned at the front of the room while lecturing or leading discussion, this physical arrangement meant that if I wore dark pants, I occasionally ended class with a white chalky stripe across my backside. I thought it amusing and wiped it off if I noticed it at all. Most students didn't care enough to say anything. A few sim-ply announce on their way out, "You've got chalk on your butt."

But one person, seeing this phenomenon for the first time, had a very different reaction. Early in a semester, one of my new students was young man who sat in the back of the room with a baseball cap pulled down so low I rarely saw his eyes. He spoke only when I took attendance, and even then only if I didn't see him tip his hat to indicate his presence in the room.

One afternoon class ended and the usual pack of students surrounded the table at the front as the rest filed out of the room. One by one they asked their questions, handed in late work, said goodbye, and left. This young man was among them, but standing back a bit and looking down at the floor. He waited until everyone else had gone, refusing to even approach my table until the last student had cleared the doorway, making for a highly awkward thirty seconds as she walked toward and out of the door.

When at last we were alone, he still didn't make eye contact, but he did approach me. He stepped closer, and then very close, and I stood still. There was something humble enough about his manner that I didn't feel threatened, just weird. Then he slowly put his head very close to mine, removed his hat and held it against his chest, and, keeping his eyes on the floor, said softly and slowly, "You might care to dust off yer britches, Ma'am."

Almost before he'd finished his sentence his hat was back on his head and he was out the door. *Britches?* I already hated being called "ma'am" everywhere I went and now I discovered I was wearing britches. I felt like I'd just walked into a Faulkner novel. I could hear this kid's Pa talking to him man-to-man in some garage or barn in rural Tennessee, "you don't ever allow a lady to be embarrassed son, and you don't look her in the eye and cause her shame. You mind your manners and show respect." I wanted to bring him a copy of "A Rose for Emily" or even *Gone With the Wind,* anything to let him know that he didn't have to do this anymore, that these were pants, thank you very much, that I was no ma'am, and that I knew all about the chalk and was fine with it. Really.

But I don't think he'd have wanted to hear it. Another time, I got a nasty black eye playing basketball, on account of my face collided violently with the back of my friend Keith's head. While sitting at a bar a few nights later, a scruffy and agitated man appeared next to me. He gripped his bottle of Miller Lite firmly and took several vigorous swigs before saying anything.

He stood there leaning on the bar next to my stool, nervously shifting his weight from one foot to the other. When he finally said hello and offered to get me a basket of free popcorn, I had no idea what he was up to. It wasn't a pick-up, to be sure. And it wasn't in any way mean.

"So," he said, pointing very briefly toward my eye before looking away again, "what are you sayin'?"

"What am I saying?" I asked. "About what?"

"About your eye."

"My eye? I'm saying I hurt it playing basketball. I tried to block my friend's lay-up but he made the basket anyway and I was running so fast that we … "

"I guess you could say that," he said, cutting me off and nodding his head.

"Well sure," I continued. I was more confused than ever but happy to tell the story, "I mean I guess I'm not very careful about the way I land when I jump and Keith, he has this way of stopping really abruptly and so … "

"Listen," he said much louder, as if I'd not been paying attention. Once he was sure I had shut up, he continued, leaning in toward me and returning to his whisper: "If your boyfriend ever comes round here, I'm gonna have to kick his ass. I don't 'preciate a man treats a woman that way."

And at that he suddenly walked away. As he settled down at a table with some friends, he seemed a calmer man. He wasn't nervous anymore, or agitated. He started flirting with a waitress and ordered himself another beer, his good deed for the day clearly accomplished.

I don't know that I've yet accounted for the sixty two million people who voted five years ago to be fleeced in the name of the very, very rich. So I'll continue with my mission. But here is my working conclusion: One marketing secret of the Republican Party, I think, is to promise American men a renewed sense of their own manliness, with all of the strength and independence that word implies in its most grossly simple, and I might add destructive form. And they get women to play along by rewarding them with lots of civility when they let their men claim sole ownership of those qualities. Sarah Palin is Florida's Katherine Harris and Minnesota's Michele Bachman rolled into one tight and perky promise: our women will do what we tell them to do, and they'll insult you until they win their right to do it!

This is an interesting strategy, and one not in keeping with traditional political advertising, because in this case, the fear being appealed to is not a fabricated one. We really are losing our strength and independence—and wages and benefits and public educational opportunities and affordable health care and security for our old age—and the people taking them away are the very ones clapping our manly men on the back and winking at our girliest women. Pretty damn clever, if you ask me.

A Mattress is a
Mattress is a Mattress

Now I know that the gap between the world depicted in advertisements and the world we really live in is wide. I know that smoking Virginia Slims won't make me a buxom secretary in a navy blue skirt suit. I know perfectly well that even the coolest looking beer bottle doesn't fill a male college student's dorm room with Playboy Bunnies competing to rip his clothes off. I know that shampooing my hair will never bring on an orgasm and that there is nothing different, or for that matter even remotely interesting, about a Dodge.

But even in the midst of all of this distortion and fabrication, the truth is that few are as strange as the peddlers of beds. The people in charge of manipulating mattress and box spring purchases speak in a language that is so utterly removed from our day-to-day, or more appropriately night-to-night lives that we cannot hope for translation. Of course beer and cigarette ads don't tell us anything useful about their products either, but at least there we're talking about impulse purchases that set one back less than $10. Sure, alcoholism and lung cancer destroy people, and sure, being destroyed is worse than having a sore neck every morning, but still, such problems are cumulative, and cannot be tied to a single purchase. The one-time mattress purchase, however, is a serious and costly commitment, and one wants to make an informed decision before agreeing to sleep on the same pile of foam and coils for ten years or more.

But instead of being able to gather useful information when we head into centers of sleep commerce or talk with their staff people, we are forced to make costly decisions using little more than the game of free association, in which you conjure up an idea randomly in response to a word or phrase written or spoken in the vicinity of a given mattress, and then go with it as if it were remotely related to the mattress being considered for purchase.

The goals that the bedding industry sets for itself are, to say the least, high. They are so high, in fact, that turning one's nose from any one of these sleep havens seems impossible. Competing mattresses promise the "world's best comfort," a "perfect night's sleep," and "pure comfort." Care to choose between those? Perhaps it would help you to know that one mattress is "America's favorite," while another is "the world's best." I don't remember the year that census workers polled us on that question—must have been too tired to answer the door that day.

One company makes you choose between two lines of beds, the *Beautyrest* and the *BackCare*. For someone such as me, whose beauty is not of the variety that needs rest, this is an easy decision—I'd opt in favor of my spine. But I imagine for those who have both backs *and* the kind of loveliness that requires substantial downtime, this is a tough call.

There is a whole line of mattresses available that promise the very same life-style upgrades the Marines promise if you join their ranks. It's good to know that there are now two ways to experience "glory," "honor," "freedom," and "independence." Wait— that's a Bush speech, and it is also true that mattress makers aren't by any means the only ones promising American glory in a mass produced product, so I guess there are lots of ways to achieve such lofty goals. I guess if you were really determined to get the best co-opted, patriotic emotional high available you could drive your

Chevy Malibu, which is in itself an "American Revolution" while listening on the radio to the president talk about anything while on your way to a military recruiting station, and then return home after enlisting just in time to collapse into your *Pillow Top Glory* bed. That's America for you. No point livin' in the land of the free if we don't make use of it every now and again.

And of course you'll want to make an informed decision regarding the foam that will inevitably be involved in the making of your mattress. Ready your critical thinking skills, so that you can distinguish precisely between *true foam*, *whisper foam*, *space foam*, *memory foam*, and, really, *zoned convoluted super soft flawless foam*. If they couldn't find a way to fix my ninety-eight-year-old Grandma's memory, why should I believe they can make a piece of foam remember anything? People make a living coming up with this crap and all I know for certain is that I chose the wrong profession.

If it's elegance that you find your life lacking the most, the mattress companies are there for you. You can buy a *Diamond*, *Sapphire*, or *Natural Response Diva* mattress. Should these names feel a bit too feminine for your manly self, why not check out the *Bravo*?

Worry that you are too frivolous during your nocturnal slumber? Maybe you're doing word-finds instead of crossword puzzles before dozing off, and then dreaming of Beyoncé concerts and Doritos? Then help yourself to the *Perfect Sleeper Cicero*. That's sure to bring on some serious profundity.

If you just plain want to feel better than everybody else, rest your superior self on the *Elite* or a *Celebrity Bed Pillow Top*. If you want to have no idea what the hell you're sleeping on, buy the *Posture Bond Chiro-Tech Ultra*, and see if you can get it with a "736 coil, unicased perimeter." At least you'll have something to wonder about as you lie there, anxiously bemoaning your rejection of your *Whisper Foam* and *Beauty Rest*.

Haunted by memories of failed spelling tests? Riddled with

anxiety over how your emails will be interpreted? Wish you could just spell it like it sounds, for godsake? Fear not, for there are beds out there for you too, my friends. For you, there is the *Stab-L Base Foundation*, the *Shock Abzzober Plus*, and mattresses offering to *Caresse* you with *Cerenity*.

There are beds with names that seem appealing to no one, but it takes all kinds I suppose. There is a boxspring made out of *Ultrasteel*, for example. I don't know what ultrasteel is, but my free association game tells me I'm supposed to intuit that it means very strong steel. And I can think of a lot of uses for steel that is particularly strong. Train tracks come to mind, and elevator shafts in very tall buildings. I suppose those huge tankers that cross the ocean could use some of this material. But under my body as I'm sleeping? No thanks.

And my favorite in the world of mattress marketing insanity is the *Nebula LX*. I don't know what the ad agency was thinking on this one, unless they thought the word sounded cool and bet that nobody would bother to look it up. A nebula can mean a mass of dust, which can't make allergy sufferers attracted to the product. Or it can mean a hazy spot on the cornea or cloudiness in urine. "Oh my, Nora, what a lovely home you have. And what's that in the bedroom next to the huge cloudy spot of urine? Is that a genuine Persian rug? It's gorgeous!"

When I furnished my first apartment, I got all of my furniture used at garage sales and junk stores, but the more reputable junk stores didn't sell used mattresses, and the ones available in people's alleys or at the stinkier junk stores weren't in any shape to be touched without rubber gloves, much less slept on, drooled on, and sat in all day with cramps or a cold. So I entered a mattress store and ran into the great wall of schlock that is the stuff of mattress marketing. I read descriptions, made note of prices, and got talked at by a relentless and highly energetic mattress salesman wearing the oxymoron of all oxymorons, a short sleeve dress shirt with a tie.

I didn't understand any of the information I gathered, except that the salesman believed from the moment he saw me that he knew precisely which mattress I should buy, and all I could think to say as I excused myself and left the store, was a quiet "yikes."

Afraid to re-enter a mattress store to investigate further, I did what research I could from home. I read a bit on the web but I couldn't get past the marketing language that had so confused me to begin with. I asked friends, but nobody knew a damned thing.

So I pulled out the phone book and called a mattress store that seemed as inconspicuous as possible. They had not bought their own half page ad in the phone book so as to scream at me, and they didn't boast about the perfect sleep or nebulas or Cicero or anything else. I appreciated the apparent lack of hype and hoped it was an indication that a normal person wearing a reasonable shirt might work there.

The place was in Maryville (pronounced "Mervul" by its residents), a small town at the foot of the Smoky Mountains, twenty miles or so south of Knoxville. The guy on the other end of the line didn't even answer with a catchy slogan, like "thanks for calling sleepland, where we work hard every day so that you can enjoy deep, satisfying sleep every night." He just picked up his probably rotary dial phone and said hello.

"Hi," I said. "I'm hoping you'll be willing to answer a question for me. I have to buy a mattress, and I've looked at a few of them but so far I can't even tell a single substantial difference between a $200 mattress and a $2,000 mattress. I mean, I don't know anything about coils and I frankly don't know whether my back feels better on firm or soft or ultrasteel and can a mattress really rest my beauty and what's true foam?"

"Ma'am?" he said.

"Oh I just don't get it, I prattled on. I mean, I don't even have $2,000 for furniture for my whole apartment but if I don't get enough coils then what will happen to me? I mean, I have to sleep on this thing every night and if I don't get beauty rest and backcare and a sapphire and Cicero with or without a pillowtop, what will happen? Will I be ugly and sore, inelegant or stupid? I'm pretty clumsy as it is, and I don't want to make it any worse by sleeping on the wrong bed. Oh jeeze. And what of the lack of abzzorbtion? What is it, if you don't mind my asking, that won't be abzzorbed if I don't buy that one? My drool or my body weight? And if I steer clear of the mattress with abzzorbtion, then do I end up with a mattress that won't abzzorb me? I mean, I just don't know what to do."

"Ma'am?" he said again, patiently.

"And I should tell you and I think I can tell you because you sound nice and you sell mattresses so you probably deal with this a lot and I'm sure everybody has to deal with it in one way or another, you see my butt is disproportionately bigger than the rest of me, and sometimes when I'm sleeping in hotels or at other people's houses I can get a sore lower back and I think it's because the mattress doesn't support my ... ."

"Ma'am!" he said more loudly, but still as sweetly as could be. "Ma'am," he said, "I want to help you."

"Hmm?" I mumbled?

He spoke so much more slowly than I did that it was hard for me to hear what he was saying. The pace of his sentence made me think he didn't understand the depth of my problem, that he wasn't paying attention, and my despair worsened, until he repeated his offer of assistance and tried more aggressively to calm me down.

"I would like to help you, ma'am, but you're going to have to *let* me help you. Will you do that for me ma'am? Would you let me help you?"

"Oh, well, sure. Thanks," I said, exhaling and letting my shoulders drop.

"Do you have a few minutes, Ma'am, so that I can really talk to you now? Can you do that for me ma'am?"

He was adamant that we slow down the tempo. It was like a basketball game between a team that likes the fast break and one that likes to slow things down and set up offensive plays that involve no fewer than seventy passes around the perimeter before making any attempt at the basket.

"Ma'am, if you will let me help you, what I want you to do is sit yourself down in a comfortable chair. Can you do that for me ma'am?"

"Oh ... well," I said, wondering how he knew I was standing. "I guess that's ok. Sure."

I slumped down into my desk chair, suspicious again that this guy was like the salesman in the store and that he was only prepping me for a new assault of nebular-posturizing-ortho-chiro talk.

But then things got interesting. He did not start talking in mattress-speak, not at all. Instead, in a voice so calm and kind he could have been singing a lullaby, he launched into a mattress exercise of sorts, the likes of which I'd never heard.

"What I want you to do, ma'am, is I want you to cloooooose yer eyes. Can you do that for me ma'am? Just clooose yer eyes for me if you can."

"Um. Right now?"

"Ma'am, I want to help you. And your gonna hafta cloooose your eyes for me, hear?"

"Ok," I said, thinking there couldn't be any danger in this. Sure, he was a stranger, and sure this was weird, but what harm could he do over the phone? I supposed he could launch into some kind of sex talk, but if that was the case I kind of wanted to hear some of it before hanging up, so I satisfied his request and closed my eyes. I'm not the sort of person who could ever lie about such a thing.

"Have you gottem closed now Ma'am?"

"I do. My eyes are closed."

I was alone in my apartment, but felt self-conscious enough to turn away from the window, so that no one outside might espy me closing my eyes on the behest of a mattress salesman in Mervul Tennessee.

"And you're in a comfortable chair, ma'am?"

"I guess. I don't really have a super comfortable chair, but this one is fine."

"Ok then. Let's get started," he said. "I want you to keep your eyes closed while I tell you something, OK Ma'am?"

"Ok. I'm ready then."

"Ma'am, what I want you to do, is I want you to picture in your mind three hundred and fifty-six mattresses."

"What?"

"That's right, Ma'am, line 'em up there in your mind. Picture three hundred and fifty-six mattresses, side by side there, all in a row. Can you do that for me?"

I tried, and I found it to be hard. "That's a lot of mattresses," I replied.

"That's right. It is a lot of mattresses. But you keep your eyes closed and get 'em all in there. You'll be able to do it, if you try."

I appreciated his faith in my mental capacity, and kept trying to line up the mattresses, until I could envision, maybe not three hundred and fifty-six exactly, but nevertheless a whole lot of mattresses lined up against a black, space-like background. They just floated there. Some had pillowtops, some had labels with grand claims writ in cursive, some were plain looking, some pink. Some were grossly thick, some looking a little thin and boring.

"Ok," I said, somewhat proud of my accomplishment. "I think I have them."

"Ma'am? What I want you to do now is I want you to keep every one of those three hundred and fifty-six mattresses in your mind so I can show you something. I want you to keep your eyes closed, hear? And keep those mattresses there in your mind."

"Ok," I said. "I'll do my best." And I really was trying. To avoid distractions I rested my forehead on the desk and squeezed my eyes closed tightly. I found it takes a high level of concentration to keep three hundred odd mattresses floating around in space in your head for any length of time.

"Still got 'em there Ma'am?"

"I do. I can see all of them."

"Do you know what you're looking at now ma'am? That's how many mattress varieties there are in the United States of America today. You've gotten all lined up there in your mind. Every one of 'em."

"Wow," I responded, impressed.

"Ok, Ma'am, now what I want you to do, is I want you to pick out just one of those three hundred and fifty-six mattresses and pull it aside."

"Just pick one?"

"That's right Ma'am. Just pick one of them mattresses and pull it aside."

"Any mattress?"

"Any which one of 'em you want to," he said. "I'm gonna show you somethin here in a minute, so pick yourself a mattress out."

And so I did. I picked a plain looking white one from near the far left end of the row, and I imagined it pulled down and set it just beneath the others, leaving a gap where it had once been.

"Ok," I said. "I've got one."

"You pick one out there, did you?" he asked. "You sure which one you picked?"

"Yes sir," I said. "I took it out of the row and put it down below, by itself."

"Good. Now Ma'am?" he continued, edging closer to his much-anticipated point. "I want you to listen to me for a minute here, won't you? What I want you to understand, Ma'am," and at this point his raised his voice and slowed down even further, "what I want you to understand Ma'am is that that there mattress you picked out ... . Well it isn't any better, and it isn't any worse, than any of them other three hundred and fifty-five mattresses that you *didn't* pick out, because Ma'am?"

"Yes?" I asked, trying not to fall over from the anticipation of it all.

"A mattress is a mattress is a mattress."

"What's that?" I stammered.

"That's right Ma'am. That there mattress you picked out isn't any different than those other mattresses you didn't pick out. That's the only thing you need to know when you're shopping for a mattress, and I want you to remember that. Do you think you can do that?"

"Oh, I said choking, "yes," "Yes sir, I can remember that. It's really a relief to learn that."

"And you want to know what else Ma'am?"

"Of course," I said, getting a hold of myself and very much wanting to know what else.

"A spring is a spring is a spring."

I was sad when our conversation was over. I loved this man. It didn't matter to me, and after fifteen years of sporadic back pain and two crappy mattresses, it still doesn't matter to me that he was absolutely wrong. In a world dominated by commercials and the liars who have to imitate them with empty promises and assurances, it is rare indeed that we meet a person who can cut directly through that thick wall of crap and say it like he thinks it is. I kept my eyes closed for a long time.

Apparently I
Know Who Satan Is

The first time it happened, my mind went blank and I swear I heard wind blowing, even though I was in a room with closed windows and doors. I had only been teaching for six or seven weeks, and though I had many of the typical new-teacher anxieties, most of them revolved around the fear that I would do something shocking or inappropriate. Obsessed with my own performance, I hadn't yet had time to worry about what students might do. So, having survived the first few weeks without having shown up naked or babbled in complete incoherency, I assumed I was in the clear. It's funny the things we assume.

I grew up in a church steeped in the values of humanism and service, much more so than it was steeped in the belief that any particular set of myths was truer than the other. I also grew up managing to avoid a lot of big books with small type, though I did, eventually, settle down and develop a serious reading habit. So I found myself a bit ill-prepared when I began teaching to groups of people who shared an impressive body of knowledge concerning the Bible.

Two years after college I started graduate work and college teaching, and I did that work at the main campus of the University of Tennessee, which is in Knoxville, which is very much in the south.

Where I'd gone to college, there were certain attributes that moved people up the social ladder. But that social system wasn't in play in Knoxville. In gas stations, grocery stores, at library counters and in classrooms, Knoxvillians don't care whether you are the son or daughter of a major advertising or banking executive, or where you house your polo ponies. Credentials like these won't help you a bit and it's likely that they'll actually diminish your chances of social approval.

This was lucky for me, as I carried no such credentials when I moved to the south. My students at UT wouldn't ever care if I was a graduate of Princeton or the University of Ballywahoo. But there was one credential I did wish I carried, and that was a serious familiarity with all things Biblical. Despite rumors I'd certainly been privy to, I was shocked to discover that for many Knoxvillians, knowledge of that book and all of its stories is part of the social contract, a necessary and assumed responsibility. I knew a lot of people claimed to believe in biblical teachings, but it never occurred to me that anyone actually read the whole book. It is a very big book and the pages are thin and the print small. And the stories are, well, a bit bizarre, especially so, I find, when we attempt to use them for navigational purposes.

At the university I had fooled enough people to become an English instructor, charged with teaching freshmen how to write papers and to read literature in an informed and intelligent way. During my first semester as an instructor of composition, I ordered a widely-used book that was organized around controversial topics, things like capital punishment, abortion, and gun control. Each chapter would showcase opposing arguments on a topic and end with writing assignments. The point of these textbooks, as far as I can tell, is to produce anxiety in students by asking them to find something new to say regarding a grossly complex issue about which there is nothing left to be said, and to do so in a handful of paragraphs and roughly two-weeks' time. What's your thesis and where are your three supporting points? Insert one paragraph showing that you understand all opposing arguments. End by briefly summing up the issue that has now been conclusively settled, thanks very much to you.

Controversial social issues initially evoke silence in classroom discussions. The only thing a typical college freshman knows about most of these well-beaten discourses is that she holds passionately-held opinions about them. That she has reached these conclusions through a process marked more by osmosis and repetition than by critical thinking does nothing to dampen the vigor of the opinion, but it does make for some reticent debaters. Nobody wants to defend their positions on this stuff, but neither do they want to hear other points of view. If I want to silence any classroom gone too far on a tangent, I can say "please give me your attention" loudly eleven times, or I can say "abortion" quietly, once.

In my Tennessee classrooms, mention of that loaded word would make the men spit chew into their Mountain Dew cans with sounds and gestures designed to indicate a warning (any simple message can be communicated with chew if the chewer is worth his snuff). The word would make the women roll their eyes and cross their arms over their chests in defiance of whatever was coming next out of the ill-informed mouth of this northern, self-righteous teacher who thought she was so charming. In my community college classes in Minnesota, uttering "abortion" leads to an instant avoidance of eye contact that is as impressive in its sophistication and variance as a southern male's tobacco chewing communication skills.

But on the whole, this silence is not hard to break, and eventually raising topics like these in writing classes leads to something else. Inevitably, it leads to unwieldy and entirely illogical discussions in which nobody, including the instructor, knows what he or she is talking about and reaching into all elements of the human experience, discussions that produce in me, above all else, the strong desire to leave the room.

Six weeks into my first semester teaching composition, I was happy to be moving from the unit on abortion, which took up a big section in our textbook. For the final period of that unit we had read an essay that mentioned the poor without access and daughters raped by fathers and women dying in alleys. Apparently, for one of the few students who had not yet spoken on the issue, this was the final straw, the assault that could not be tolerated, and so he added his voice to the chorus of unreasonable arguments that had become my classroom. He raised his fist in the air and shouted *"why should the mother get to choose whether or not to be poor or be raped or not and die and not the baby?"* I looked right at him, listening to the surge of supportive grunts and offended gasps sweeping through the room. It was clear that every student was about to start talking at the same time, some with closed eyes brimming over with tears and some with what appeared to be claws extending out toward the speaker. I considered the odds of us ever getting back to paragraph structure, and I let the class go early. So I was thrilled to wrap up that unit and head into the next section of the textbook, which promised to provide opposing points of view on another subject about which none of us was qualified to argue: women in combat. After two weeks of listening to my students' hysterical rages on the topic of when life does or does not begin, the papers had been handed in and that was that.

Since the topic of women in combat was debated in the nineties on both sides more often with reason than hysteria, and since my students did not feel the issue was one over which they were compelled to wage duels or to weep openly, I felt more confident in my ability to advocate, as it goes, for the devil in this new unit, and to keep our primary focus on argumentation. And class went smoothly for a week and a half. We read predictable essays on the problem of sexual activity breaking and not breaking down morale, on women's capacity for soldierly work, and on equality and fairness. We were calm people, capable of respect and new ideas.

My sense of relief was palpable. On the fourth and final day of our consideration of the topic, we were reviewing an essay whose sole purpose was to define "combat." Relative to the territory previously trodden by our class, the issue was so benign that I was more relaxed than I had been yet as a teacher, even fancying myself competent.

But suddenly it happened, about thirty minutes into the discussion. A young man in the middle of the room stood up, arms at his sides, eyes fixed above my head and far away, and began to speak with impressive annunciation and passion. At first I thought there was some kind of emergency, that he'd seen a car accident out of the window or that he was announcing the onset of his own major heart attack. But as he spoke, I got increasingly muddled.

"But if any provide not for his own, and specially for those of his own house, he hath denied the faith, and is worse than an infidel!"

My mind came up with no possible explanations and was left a blank space filled with only whiteness and wind. When he finished his declaration, or whatever it was, he lowered his eyes to mine and barked as if in a Marine drill, "First Timothy Chapter Five Verse Eight!" and then, apparently fighting the urge to salute somebody not in the room, promptly sat down.

One book I had managed to read and promptly forget as an undergraduate was Milton's *Paradise Lost.* In another class, I'd been asked to read the Gospel of Matthew, and did manage to procure a Bible from a motel room so that I might do just that, but I never carried through on those intentions. I knew the Christmas story because despite our church's lack of Christian ideology, we produced a fine Christmas pageant each year. So I knew a few things. I knew who Moses was, roughly, and I knew quite a bit about Mary and Joseph, and Adam and Eve. The rest of it, however, was news to me.

Had Tim's outburst occurred during our abortion discussions,

I would have ended the class immediately and waited for the unit to go away. But I had something at stake here. A feeling, if fleeting, of confidence had been mine only moments before, and we'd begun to look like a college class. I wasn't ready to give that up, so I decided to stick it out and see what a little fraudulent bravado might accomplish. I acted as one deep in thought rather than in a white, windy vacuum, and offered every teacher's ace in the hole. "Wow Tim, a very interesting set of implications there. Go ahead and explain for the others how this pertains to Vella's definition of combat."

But Tim would say nothing. He sat rigidly in his chair, arms folded across his chest, and looked at me like I was an idiot. Another student finally challenged him, raising my hopes for coherence, connection, plain sense, but she only wanted to argue that what had been said was not the be all and end all of the Lord's teachings on female soldiers, saying only, "Ephesians says the same thing." Class ended early again.

By the end of the semester two more students had offered vigorous and random biblical recitations, and I came to expect them. I also quickly learned that there was never going to be a follow up. An outburst like this functioned like the period at the end of a sentence, a moment of punctuation guided by rules someone else had established and that my students understood. I grew to accept these moments as one might fire drills or sudden and inexplicable nausea, as one of the many things that happen without warning and that mean class is finished for the day.

After a few years teaching, I got to know some of my students well enough to ask them about this phenomenon. They had grown up in southern evangelical churches, the kinds of places where preachers wore power packs on their belts so that they could move among the congregants, allowing no teenager comfort or safety from the hellfire and damnation stories flowing from the surround sound speakers. One student later told me that everything he'd ever learned about abortion and gun control he had learned in church, where the game was to find the Biblical passage that contained God's final decision on the matter and then offer it up, thus closing the discussion and solving the controversy.

Realizing that in two short months I was not going to be successful inserting the rules that logic and critical thinking demand into their well-honed, Bible-passage problem-solving skills, I learned to make the most of my situation. Reading the Bible might have been a good place to start, but I didn't see the point of that since I really didn't want to and could be guaranteed to always have biblical experts in the room. Yet another person spontaneously reciting Corinthians in the middle of class discussions didn't seem necessary, and besides, how could I ever catch up with these guys?

So I did two things to make my life easier: In composition classes, I stopped using textbooks that took us into random controversial subjects, opting instead for books that were actually about how to write papers. I never did elicit a spontaneous Bible recitation while offering an overview of Aristotle's *Rhetoric*. Secondly, I created spaces in my literature classes for biblical experts to lend us some of their wisdom in a controlled, more predictable fashion.

Since American literature is heavily influenced by Christian thought, my lack of biblical familiarity created problems on a regular basis. When teaching a short story that invoked Christian imagery, I was used to staying up a little longer the night before to look the reference up in encyclopedias and biblical glossaries so that if anyone asked, I'd know at least minimally what the reference was about. Then I'd cruise through class spending time on every other element of the story, knowing I had at least a sentence prepared if the reference came up. This is a fine way to get through a fifty-minute class period, but not a very fine way to read stories that rely on biblical passages to impart their most serious messages.

Once I figured out that some of my students already commanded a vast body of knowledge that I both lacked and needed,

I stopped with the extra preparation the night before class. Instead, I wrote in my class notes a simple phrase: "Ask for someone to tell the story of Job." Students would compete for the privilege of responding, having clearly been rewarded in the past for knowing these stories intimately. A few times, two students raised their hands at once, and then all would look at me to see who would be chosen for the honor. And the competition didn't end with my selection. If any detail was left out in the telling of the story, other students would quickly charge into the now-shamed territory to fill in the gap.

This process of competitive Bible recitation would take up enough class time for me to formulate an idea of how the Christian image related to the text we were looking at, and by the time they had exhausted their memories of details and sorted out any disagreements, I usually had the reference figured out and could lead us back to the story, now made richer for all of us. In this way I completed my first really thorough, close readings of countless short stories, poems, and novels. There are visual learners and kinesthetic learners. I've discovered I'm a have-your-students-explain-it-to-you-over-and-over-again learner.

Since I knew that geography was one of the biggest factors in determining how many biblical passages were likely to be flowing through my students' heads, I should have paid more attention when I left Tennessee and moved back to Minnesota for a teaching job at a community college. Done with graduate school, I was pretty full of myself, finished with new-teacher anxieties and confident in my ability to milk necessary information from my students to make sense of a story or poem on the spot.

Early in the first semester at my new job, one of my classes read Faulkner's "Barn Burning," a story that draws so overt a picture of Satan that even I could catch it. After all, by then I'd heard no fewer than thirteen previous students point out the similarity between the character in Faulkner's story and the one in Christian tales. As usual, I failed to brush up on the story or look anything up the night before class, and wrote in my class notes, "If nobody points it out, ask for someone to tell the story of Satan's fall from grace."

In class, I ploddingly called their attention to the various elements of Faulkner's character that allude overtly to the devil, waiting for some student to catch on, start reciting, and take over for a while so that I could think things through. When that didn't happen naturally, I followed the directions in my notes and stood back to see who would win the fight to tell the story. Not only did no one begin reciting or explaining, but nobody would make eye contact with me. There were thirty-five students in the room, and the thirty-four who were awake were actively averting their eyes. They were suddenly, it seemed, interested in the time, tying their shoes, and getting lipstick out of their purses. One woman got up and left the room. Even the best students, the ones who could be counted on to answer every question, took to writing notes with such concentration you'd think they just had the most revelatory idea of their lives and had to write it down right now or lose it forever.

"Please. Somebody tell us the story of Satan's fall from grace. Come on guys, participation is a requirement in this class."

Nothing.

"Are you serious? Somebody tell us the story of Satan's fall from grace."

Nothing again, followed by a full, painful minute of no response whatsoever. Finally, out of the silence of my indignation and their embarrassment, a young man in the back who could no longer bear it spoke. He hesitated, gripped his hair with his fist as if to rip it out in exasperation, and grimaced as he responded:

"Didn't he, well jesus, I dunno. But I think, well, didn't he, like, piss off god or something?"

Again I heard wind, and again my mind went blank with surprise.

The students were instantly relieved that the silence was broken, and they relaxed their shoulders and stopped looking for a clock that was not on the wall behind them. Almost all of them began to write the information down in their notebooks (Satan=bad, pissed off God). Some students appeared genuinely interested in the adventures of this guy … what'd you say his name was—Satan? What did he do—kill somebody?

I tried to close my mouth and think of what to say next. Were they seriously asking *me* this? I felt like Dorothy lost on the yellow brick road and knowing for the first time how good she had it back in Kansas. There I was, the one person in a room of more than thirty who knew the most about a figure as substantial (shadow-casting powers notwithstanding) as Satan. Mourning my obvious loss, I imagined what my students in Tennessee would say if they were here to tell his story.

And as I stood there dreaming of a different classroom nine-hundred miles away, a new door creaked open in my brain. Inside, I saw a whole host of stories I didn't know were there. And to my great surprise I saw that some of them starred the fellow my students were asking about. There, Satan's fall from grace played itself out in surprising detail—there was God's uppity angel, the one who aspired to overtake the big guy himself, being cast out with all of his lesser angels. And I saw tangential stories too. There he was later, double daring God to test Job's faith, and there again tempting God's kid to do the wrong thing.

So, shocking nobody more than myself, I told my students a few stories. They asked questions, and I knew the answers to a handful of them. I was even able to tell them that Isaiah would be a good place for them to start if they wanted to look into the matter on their own. I did not tell them that if they did not want to look into it on their own, they could instead spend seven years in a classroom in Tennessee. As they left the room at the end of the period, I considered the years of teaching that rolled out ahead of me—years of teaching Faulkner and Douglass, Dickinson and Hawthorne, Eliot and O'Connor and so many more—and I knew that I wasn't so very hopeless after all.

Roy and
the Toilet Teddy

Within twenty miles, give or take, of Black Mountain, North Carolina, just off an Interstate 40 exit, is a motel that appears from without and within to be much like any other cheaply-made motel in the area. It offers scratchy synthetic linens and towels, lots of noise, and a funky smell. I don't recommend it to anyone.

All old motels have stories to tell—they must—but it's rare that we get many clues about what kinds of human dramas worked themselves out there. Whether seedy or marginally slick, motels hold their secrets tightly. You can almost hear the fights, the raucous parties, the despair, the break-ups, the betrayals, the abuse, and the ennui that were held by the walls before you came. You can guess at the cause of the scant physical clues left behind, a carpet stain, a gash in the furniture, or a torn shower curtain, but the uniform rooms refuse to spill, making you feel not only an outsider, but a late one at that.

I find that disconcerting. It's the same feeling I get when I'm trying to work in old and storied libraries. Vanderbilt has a library like that, and I don't know how anyone can get work done in a place where so many great thoughts have preceded them. I need newer structures in which to think, places built at the latest in the 1950s. It doesn't matter to me if they are particularly nice places, but I can't be expected to have creative ideas at desks where too

116

many brilliant people have had unknown epiphanies and intellectual breakthroughs. Hundred-year-old oak library tables are lovely to look at but they seem to me too proud of their previous accomplishments. Snobby, really.

On a weekend trip to Asheville, North Carolina, an artsy college town near the Tennessee border, my girlfriend and I waited too long to start looking for a place to stay. Forgetting that Asheville can draw huge crowds, we didn't think about a motel until dinner and several hours at a bar were behind us. We discovered that the rooms in the city were all full, as were the rooms in the motels on the interstate leading into and out of the city. So we kept driving east looking for vacancy signs until finally, past eleven, we landed at this nondescript place on the far side of Black Mountain.

Yes, said the guy watching television behind the counter, they had one room left, and the price was high because what choice did we have, and as we left the little office area, the guy left with us, closing up shop and turning off the lights before getting into his truck and driving away. We trudged down the dirty sidewalk in front of the rooms until we got to ours, and beheld, not surprisingly, a fairly nasty old motel room. What we didn't know at the time was that this motel room would prove far more willing than most to divulge its secrets.

The night was not a restful one. My girlfriend and I were kept awake first by the sounds of large amounts of rushing water coming from the toilet, which was running badly. Neither of us could sleep with these sounds of toilet turbulence, but neither of us necessarily felt it our duty to open it up to investigate. It was enough to get used to the funky smell and the prickly sheets without having to pry too far into the workings of the bathroom and its fixtures.

Holding out hope that my girlfriend would be irritated enough to solve the problem herself, I searched for a comfortable position in the uncomfortable bed while pressing a foul-smelling pillow over my head to block out the noise. When that didn't work, I tried to trick my imagination into thinking that I was camping and that the noise was that of a creek winding down the mountain just beside our campsite.

I had lived for a year in an apartment complex next to married people who were forever screaming at each other late at night. The only thing I could do to sleep through the ruckus was turn my radio on loudly and to tune it to pure, swishing static. Then I'd think of a mountain stream and eventually sleep through their arguments. Toilets make for worse mountain streams than radios do, though, at least when accompanied by funky smells and bad linens, and my trick was of no use this time. My girlfriend tossed back and forth, irritated indeed, though no more willing to engage with the toilet problem than I.

Then came the pounding and the screaming. It was just after one in the morning, and we'd each been silently wrestling with the damned toilet noise for nearly two hours. When the lady first pitched her body into the door, we jumped out of bed. My heart was racing, it seemed, before I was even aware of what was happening, and I ran to the door and jammed my foot against it. My girlfriend stood back by the bathroom, facing the door as if about to perform some kind of Kung Fu defensive move.

There was a woman outside our door hell bent on getting inside of it. She had a scratchy voice and she was screaming as she flung her body at the door and rattled the doorknob.

Neither of us could think of anything to say or do, so we remained frozen in our defensive positions and stared at the puny door lock that we'd worried about at bedtime. There was no deadbolt, just a doorknob lock button that you pushed in, like the kind you'd expect in a McDonald's bathroom stall. The door itself was hollow and flimsy and more appropriate for closets than an external doorway.

Three things were clear about the woman at our door: she was very drunk, she was convinced that a man named Roy was in our room, and she felt strongly that Roy had better come and open the door right now goddammit. She didn't think much of this

Roy at the moment, either. It was hard to tell precisely what she was saying, not because of the thickness of the door or walls that separated us—breezes came right through those—but rather because she kept losing her train of thought and twice fell down in mid-sentence, the second time breaking into song while on the ground and seeming to forget her purpose altogether.

When standing and on track, she pitched herself violently over and over again at the door but did not succeed in opening it. This should have but did not give me more faith in paper thin doors with puny door knob locks on them: "Roy! You sonabitch, I know you're in there. Open the goddamned door Roy you sonabitch. Imma tell Marilyn about you Roy. You goddamned know I will you sonabitch. Roy!" Wham! Came another pitch into the door, accompanied by hostile rattling of the doorknob. "Open the goddamned door Roy!"

Well, what with how hard her body was hitting the door and what with how unlikely it seemed that she would even notice that we weren't Roy if she saw us, we didn't open the door and were shocked that she didn't either. We considered opening it during one of her "rests" on the pavement, but figured even if she recognized that we weren't Roy, she was likely to consider us sonabitches nevertheless, being in such a foul mood and all.

After her second fall, during which she'd conducted her own singing with dramatic hand gestures in the air above her body, she got up and continued her threats and demands and shook the door a few more times (we peeked through the curtains easily without notice—I don't guess her peripheral vision was terribly keen that night). Then she staggered to the back of the parking lot where she belted out her threats to Roy while leaning heavily against the side of a car, presumably to lessen her risk of falling on her ass. From there, her pleas became less hostile and more vulnerable. "You know I love ya Roy. You know that's the truth. Open the goddamned door Roy!" Soon, though, she was back to her wrestling match with our door.

My girlfriend dialed "0" on the phone by the bed several times, but we knew there was nobody in the office to pick it up. We didn't consider calling the police because, well, because we were lesbians in the hills of North Carolina near the Tennessee state line, and such people generally like to keep a very low profile.

I don't know why nobody else in the motel called the police, for certainly nobody slept through it. After all, the woman sounded even less like a mountain stream than our toilet did. Perhaps they thought it amusing or just sad and, noting her specific fixation on our door, found nothing threatening in it.

When finally, after forty minutes or so, she went away and stayed away, I remained by the door with my foot wedged at the bottom of it, leaning over to peer out the window for still another twenty minutes, sweating and trying to calm my heart rate down.

At quarter to three we decided to try once again to get some sleep, but as soon as we stopped our frenetic and cathartic re-enactments of the woman's threats and our own door-blocking, martial-arts-themed defenses, the damned toilet noise rushed into the newly formed relative silence and filled it up again.

This time I was pissed enough to not care so much about the fact that the toilet looked old and nasty. I wanted it quiet, and after failing to come up with an appropriate response to the violent woman at our door, in fact after failing to come up with any response whatsoever, I needed a problem I could solve. Toilets aren't all that complicated, after all, and so I yanked the porcelain lid off the back of the commode and looked around.

The problem was obvious. There was a rag or a cloth of some sort jamming up the hole at the bottom so that the plugging device could not create a seal and the toilet could never sufficiently fill. But I couldn't reach the cloth without sticking my hand in the water, something that, despite my newfound need for bravery, I really didn't want to do. So I fished for it with whatever I could find for a while, using part of a broken towel rack and a wire hanger. But the cloth wouldn't budge. A large enough portion of it had been sucked down the hole that I eventually had to roll up my sleeve and take the plunge.

By then it was 3:30 or so, and I was crabby and still scared and now completely grossed out. I was in a cheap motel in the middle of nowhere without good locks or good blankets and my hand was inside a toilet filled with murky water.

I grabbed the cloth and with a strong yank pulled up the offending blockage. In an effort to get it as far from my body as possible, I held it up and away from me, which, unfortunately, allowed water to run down my arm and into my sweatshirt. And there is nothing quite like the feel of toilet water running down one's torso in a funky smelling motel room far from home.

I fumbled with the thing and tried in vain to find a place to fling it (I intended to brush my teeth in the sink, for godsake, and the garbage can was made of metal mesh and would not hold the water). I managed only to splatter water all over the scruffy linoleum floor and made the problem worse instead of better. While I flailed about, my girlfriend let out a shriek. She wasn't worried about my rather disgusting predicament, but rather was focused on the thing itself, the identity of which I hadn't yet had time to care about. Noting her shock and subsequent laughter, I stopped flailing and let part of it drop from my fist.

As it unfolded itself in the air I saw what we were dealing with: a red satin teddy trimmed with black lace, one that was puckered and twisted from toilet water pressure and torn in one armpit, but a teddy nonetheless.

This, I thought, is one hell of a motel room. The place was beginning to crack and tell us a few things. But what, exactly, was it saying? We looked outside and saw no sign of the woman who'd been at our door. So I took a shower and used all of the soap I could find, which was the motel kind that doesn't seem to want to rinse off, and then we slept for a few hours with only the relatively distant noise of the interstate to contend with.

Exhausted but happy to be free, we sat the next morning in a Waffle House, trying to put the pieces of the previous night together. And while I understand that it's possible that drunken woman had the wrong room, maybe even the wrong motel, hell, maybe she didn't even know it was a motel and thought she was at Roy's house, I prefer to think that she knew precisely where she was. I prefer to think that she could have, in a more steady frame of mind, told us a thing or two about the toilet teddy and its relationship to Roy and/or said Marilyn.

What set of events would lead a sane person to throw a perfectly good teddy into the back of a toilet? I don't even know what set of events would lead a perfectly sane person to buy a teddy in the first place, but I'm willing to skip over that one in the spirit of diversity. And what set of events could have led to the woman beating on our door as she did?

Here's my guess. And I'll add before I offer this that should anyone out there know more about Roy, Marilyn, drunken lady, or the teddy, please write me a letter as soon as you are able. I will also say that if you know not a thing about these folks or Black Mountain, North Carolina but have a plausible story that links them all together, well I'd like to know that too.

But here's what I think. I think it wasn't luck that we found the only empty motel room within thirty miles of Asheville. And I think the teddy incident was recent.

Supporting Argument Number One: nobody cleaning the room could have missed the noise of water pouring down the drain of the toilet, and as the place was probably run by only one or two people, it's likely the room cleaner had an interest in the size of his or her utility bills and that the easily-fixable problem, therefore, would not have been ignored for long.

I'm going to go out on a limb here and surmise that Roy was the previous occupant of the room and that Roy had a visitor, let's call her for the sake of argument, well, drunken lady. And I think this visitor and Roy had a thing going on, a thing not unlike the things that go on in cheap and expensive motels and hotels world-wide. I think that Roy's visitor got dressed and left the room for a time, perhaps to tend to her voracious appetite for alcohol.

Supporting Argument Number Two: She was really smashed the one time I saw her and she appeared practiced in the art of being smashed, what with being so comfortable on the pavement that she broke out into song and what with knowing how to prop herself up on cars and all.

I think that when Roy's visitor left the room, she left behind a particular item of clothing, a little number she'd purchased, let's say the weekend before, in hopes of surprising her beloved for his birthday, or their anniversary, or, more likely, in hopes of winning him back from the clutches of his, yep, his wife Marilyn.

I think drunken lady and Roy had a fight, a fight over whether or not Roy was indeed going to leave Marilyn for drunken lady, as had been promised for years upon years, as is so often the case in these cases. I think the teddy marked the last straw for drunken lady, a kind of ultimatum loaded with all the sexiness her aging and alcoholic body could muster, and I think that it didn't work, that Roy had his fun, got up, and declared his intention to return to his wife.

So drunken lady left in a rage, and headed straight for the local alcohol trough, yoked herself to it until she felt numb, and then drank some more until she eventually started to feel brave and capable of great things.

Supporting Argument Number Three: drunken lady was desperate, and her threat to reveal Roy's secrets to Marilyn should be read in that light. She'd only have told Marilyn about their tryst if it were her last option for forcing Roy's hand. If he couldn't be seduced into leaving his wife, then he'd have to be kicked out by his enraged wife. It was a risk, she knew, but drunken lady had to threaten him with something.

Meanwhile, Marilyn, tipped off by a neighbor who had been at the local bar and heard drunken lady's tirade, headed straight

for the local motel, where she'd long suspected Roy had been host-
ing a floozy. He'd taken less care, over the years, to hide the affair,
parking his car now directly in front of the room, easily visible
from the exit ramp. Even he couldn't say whether he wanted his
wife to find out and stop the affair or whether he enjoyed the
power of flaunting his unseemly behavior for all to see.

Supporting Argument Number Four: well, I don't have any,
but use your imagination just a little, will you?

Seeing his wife's car pull into parking lot, Roy looked around
the room and panicked when he saw the only colorful thing in it:
the red and black teddy. Having five seconds to work with, he
flung it in the only place he could think to fling it—the back of
the toilet.

Supporting Argument Number Five: Exhibit A, the teddy, was
found in that very same toilet later in the same evening.

Supporting Argument Number Six: When I was near the bathroom needing quickly to find a place to dump Exhibit A so as to
stop getting toilet water on my person, I couldn't find anything
other than the back of the toilet, from which I'd snatched it. The
only other place to conceal the teddy would have been the empty
drawers, but that's too likely a place for a pissed off and long suspicious wife to miss, and Roy, though desperate, was no fool.

I think that Marilyn then found her man easily enough. I
think she confronted him as any fed-up and had-just-about-
enough-of-this woman would have done. He confessed and offered to end the thing. Roy, who never wanted to leave his wife in
the first place which is the same reason drunken lady was at that
very moment getting drunk, professed his undying love for
Marilyn, told her of the ruthless seduction by drunken lady, and
made love to her right there on the very same bed. I think the two
of them decided to go home, holding hands and cooing at one
another before getting in their separate cars, feeling as if they'd
just washed themselves of the pain of this affair with the kind of
soap that does, actually, rinse off.

And I think the motel owner, noting the newly vacated room and aware that the market was ripe on this particular weekend, figured he could clean it fast and make a quick fifty bucks before heading home.

So motel guy changed the bedding and towels and put new bars of non-rinseable soap on the sink. He brought the dirty linens to the cleaning cart on the sidewalk and returned to the room a final time to empty the garbage can. Seeing in it nothing but a wadded up Kleenex, likely soiled during drunken lady's tearful remonstrations with Roy the still-devoted husband, motel guy, being a lazy fellow, elected to dump the minor contents of the trashcan into the toilet rather than carrying the whole thing out to the cart. He flushed the toilet, gave the room a final glance to make sure all was well, and left before hearing the toilet fail to fill. Motel guy then returned to his office and flicked on the television just in time for me and my girlfriend, fresh from the bars in Asheville, to pull up with a VISA card that happened to be in perfectly good condition. And the rest of the story, well I've already told you that.

For the Wife of Bath and the Wife of Yeats, I Give Thanks

When students are preparing to take major exams in graduate school English departments, they don't pay heed to a great many wives. Before we enter the room in which our knowledge of the English and American canons is to be tested, whether in writing or through conversation with those whose knowledge is already firmly established, we pay much attention to books and to their writers and assume that the topic of wives is about as likely to come up as is the topic of apricots.

Sure, we are aware that some of the writers were wives, and some of them had wives. On our way into such rooms, for example, we are likely to be aware that a lot of the writers we are prepared to talk about didn't get the wives they wanted and that Ernest Hemingway got more of them than he wanted. We are aware that Hester's problem in *The Scarlet Letter* is that she was not properly wived and that everybody except Emily Dickinson seems to think that this was her problem, too. We know that T.S. Eliot's wife went nuts, and as we've read the *Four Quartets*, we are not surprised by this. And we know that no writer has ever loved having a wife as much as Gertrude Stein. In the main, though, such details are extraneous to our primary focus.

The greatest exception to this rule is a character writ by Geoffrey Chaucer known as the Wife of Bath. Both the character herself and her wifely status loom importantly in the field and any student sufficiently prepared for these exams is ready to talk about her.

This particular wife from a place called Bath enjoys herself immensely and is just plain fun to be around. Her name is Alison, and in *The Canterbury Tales*, she uses her experiences with five husbands to support her argument that sex is good and virginity overrated. About this subject she waxes on for some time. Even better, she makes waste of the myth that men ought to be in charge of everything, a clear indication that not enough people in charge today have read their Chaucer. She's saucy, and I like her.

Alison marries husband #5 who is a pretty young fellow and seems nice, only to discover after they are married that he's one of those guys who wears his undershirt around the house and enjoys regular bouts of slapping his wife upside the head. As he does so, he is particularly fond of reading aloud from a book written by the fourteenth century ancestors of Rush Limbaugh, Andrew Dice Clay, and Howard Stern, about how stupid, awful, and dangerous women are.

The method by which Alison trumps husband #5 and teaches him his lesson is somewhat troubling by today's standards, but it hardly seems fair to judge her that way. Fed up, she rips his book apart and tosses him into the fire. He recovers, rages, and hits her head so hard she remains forever deaf in one ear. She pretends to be dead, winning his remorse and a pledge of nonviolence. Then for good measure she hits him again, winning his agreement that from now on, she'll be the one in charge, thank you very much.

All of which is kind of cathartic in the same way a talk show is cathartic for its viewers. The outrageous teenagers or abusive fathers get to come on stage and strut their crude, uncaring stuff, but at the end of the show, as we all know, their victims will muster up some kind of defiance and, most importantly, the audience will get their chance to scream at the self-proclaimed freaks on stage, making everybody at home feel, well, better about their own, comparatively normal lives.

But still, The Wife of Bath is probably not a good advice manual for women in abusive relationships. After all, once the show's over, the self-righteous audience goes home and the victim has to face her abuser alone. Thanks to millions of accounts of men like husband #5 we've read since this one, we now know a bit more than Chaucer did about this husband's remorse and how much we ought or ought not to rely on his repentance. By now we've come to be more than a little suspicious when a fellow says to his bruised and bleeding beloved, "As help me God, I shal thee nevere smyte."

And so we wince when dear Alison believes him and lets him stick around. But given that Alison is likely to have seen far fewer public service announcements and billboards urging battered women to get out than the rest of us, I forgive her this dangerous and ill-informed move. She didn't know any better. You deal with what you've got, you know what I mean?

Anyway, Chaucer's Alison is a woman to be reckoned with, and the point is that if you're taking a major exam on English literature, you know who she is.

After two years spent preparing for graduate school and two more in graduate school doing little more than reading and re-reading books, I prepared to take my master's exams. We had to take a written exam first, to prove we were in the ballpark, and then an oral exam, to prove that we would not soil our pants under great pressure and thereby bring shame to the field. During both exams all questions regarding American and British litera-ture were fair game. Holding Beowulf and Oscar Wilde and Mark Twain and Toni Morrison and everyone in between in one's head all at the same moment is not an easy thing to do, let me tell you, especially if one's head is about the size of mine.

But I was ready. I made it through the written exam fine, except for the minor problem of forgetting the name of the heroine in a novel called *Mrs. Dalloway*. So throughout an eighty-minute essay I wrote over and over again about "the heroine in Mrs. Dalloway." It was only on my way home later that day that I remembered her name actually was Mrs. Dalloway. The faculty reading the written exams may have gotten a laugh, but they didn't hold it against me, and I was cleared to select my orals committee.

My committee was made up of my Chaucer professor, my feminist theory professor, my Renaissance poetry professor, and my nineteenth-century novel professor. As I asked each of them to participate, as I reviewed all of my notes, as I showered that morning, and as I sweated with near panic on my way into the room that day, I fully assumed that the primary question of the day involved how things would go for me. If that sounds a little self-interested, it was. From my perspective, which was the only one available to me at the time, the day's single and great significance was that it was the day on which I might have failed attempting to do the only thing I really wanted to do with my life. It never occurred to me that the day might go poorly for anybody else, or that I might profit from such a turn of events.

But profit I did, and here's how it went. When we got started, my Chaucer professor, being a very kind person, began the questioning by asking about something she knew I knew. In fact, she had just finished reading a paper I'd written on the topic. She asked me to talk a little bit about the Wife of Bath.

This should have been a sweet moment. It should have been the moment that the cloud of tension which had been hovering over my head for weeks floated away in the cool breeze. It should have been the moment I realized I was fine, that I started talking intelligently, that I impressed myself and the committee, and charged ahead like I'd intended to.

But it wasn't. Because the gods must be both crazy and mean, when Chaucer professor asked me who the wife of Bath was, the only thing I could envision was white space. My recollection of dear Alison and husband #5 was completely gone, wiped away in a moment.

I squirmed in my chair and held my mouth open, so that should a thought come to me, I'd be ready to spit it out quickly. But nothing came. Where only an hour before there had been confessional poems and slave narratives and sonnets and one-act plays, now there was nothing. And the white space wasn't light and airy either. What I saw in my head were dirty white walls. It was like being in a small windowless museum gallery with all the paintings taken down. There were smudge marks and faded lines outlining the spots where the paintings had hidden the walls from dirty hands and light, but the paintings themselves were gone, as were the little white cards on which were written the names of the artists, the titles, and brief synopses of the significance of the works.

The Chaucer professor felt badly—she'd only wanted to help after all, and what more could a person do than ask about a character the student has just finished writing about? So she tried to stop the hemorrhaging, and asked me to simply identify Chaucer himself. After all, that's all she and I had talked about for the past two months. It was an embarrassingly easy softball of a question, but it didn't help. I had no idea what she was talking about and could think of nothing to say.

The cloud of tension over my head was gaining in density and ferocity, and it appeared more and more like a cloud of doom than of mere tension. This was the end, I thought. It all stops here. Right here on this stupid plastic chair in this old office, I've been undone by somebody calling herself the Wife of Bath. I scanned the horizons of my memory in desperation, but could think of not a single thing that was ever written by anybody. There was just nobody home.

The cloud rumbled, threatening to strike at any time, and I wished I had brought an umbrella or that I had at least had the foresight to sit closer to the door.

I couldn't look anyone in the eye, so taken was I by the white walls crowding up my consciousness. I could only hear the hum of failure in the air. I felt naked with self-consciousness.

Finally, nineteenth-century novel professor decided he'd have to act. He seemed to think I was still worth one last rescue attempt. Rather suddenly he leaned back and exhaled, as if to relieve the tension for all of us, and said in a lighter, easier voice than the situation called for, "well, let's talk about Yeats, then."

I was surprised by this question which came from a man who spoke far more often of Charles Dickens, George Eliot, and Wilkie Collins, not that those names would have meant anything to me at the moment. So surprised, in fact, that something inside of me shook loose, which I suppose was the intent of the question. The white walls didn't go away, but the room they encased became slightly cluttered. And among the clutter was a poet by the name of Yeats. An Irish guy. I knew that. Hey!, I thought, I know something! The guy is Irish! I didn't see much, but the slight improvement gave me hope enough to raise my gaze from the floor and look at this kind man, my nineteenth-century novel professor.

"Yeah," I said. "Ok. Let's talk about Yeats."

"What can you tell me about Yeats' gyre theory?" he asked.

I looked around in my mental gallery some more, only slightly more hopeful, and was shocked to see Yeats' gyre there sitting on the floor of the room.

"Well," I said. "He had this idea, see, that western culture was finished with something, Christianity, maybe, and that we were turning further and further away from what held us together before."

I sat back in my chair, looking at the geometrical shape that was Yeats' gyre, now fully developed in my mind. I continued. "Turning and turning in the widening gyre, the falcon cannot hear the falconer."

I smiled because I knew most of the rest of the poem was there too, because I knew something about that poem and the

guy who wrote it and what he was getting at and why we still read
it. My shoulders relaxed and everybody in the room sighed a col-
lective sigh of relief. I was not quite finished, after all.

At least not yet.

After I went on for some time about Yeats and his gyre theory
and modern thinking and how god was dead and all the poets
thought they'd write the new religion and all of that, after I'd talked
for some time, feeling more and more like a human being, Renaissance poetry guy piped up.

Now the tone was changed. The committee members, seeing
that I was back in the game, switched from emergency techni-
cians trying to keep me alive into the fairly tenacious examiners
they had come into the room in the first place to be.

Renaissance guy's tone did not suggest he was throwing a softball. And he wasn't trying to change the subject to see if he could
get me on a more productive track.

"And where," he asked somewhat threateningly, "did Yeats *get*
this idea for the gyre?"

He sat smugly in his chair, arms newly folded across his chest.

I sank again into humiliation. I'd been moving so nicely along
the tracks for such a short period of time, and then this guy had to
go and ask where someone had gotten the big idea. I hadn't studied where people got their ideas. I had studied the ideas, and that
had seemed like a lot at the time.

"I don't know," I said, returning my gaze to the floor and
slouching down in my chair. I felt the dark cloud descend to en-
gulf me, and I was ready to accept defeat.

It's important to note that by this point in the exam, the only
person who had not yet spoken was feminist theory professor, by
far the most aggressive personality in the room. During the Sara-
appears-to-be-brain-dead phase of my exam, she'd sat back and let
the other more nurturing members of the team ply their people skills.
I wasn't looking up to know, but my guess is that she raised her eyebrows and looked at her watch several times during that episode.

Feminist theory professors in the nineties were aggressive by nature. They had to be to survive as scholars in a field that prided itself on nastiness, and besides, they were the embodiment of an ongoing battle between an older canon examined in traditional ways and something altogether new. The only two things guaranteed about English departments during this period were that they had at least one such person on their faculty rosters, and that some other faculty members did not like what that person stood for. So feminist theory professors walked around and wrote their books as if ready for assault.

Well Renaissance guy was no feminist scholar, that's to be sure, and he and feminist theory professor were good examples of the great divide that split many an English department during that decade. He was a man studying old dead guys. She was a woman with the gall to suggest that there was more to it than that. One had tradition on his side. One had a chip on her shoulder big enough to house Anita Hill, the witches of Salem, and the Wife of Bath herself, not to mention characters and stories and poems written by actual women. These two colleagues weren't intellectual soul-mates, if you know what I mean, though they got along fine at social gatherings as long as there was enough wine to go around.

Anyway, back to my moment of doom. When I ceded the question about where Yeats got his idea, nobody jumped in to carry the conversation forward. So Renaissance guy provided the answer to his own question, I suppose so that I could be better educated on my way into a career in the fast food industry. Nice of him, I guess, though I don't know as the origins of Yeats' gyre theory dominate the conversations over the drive-thru headset airwaves.

"Well he got it," Renaissance guy said with a huff, as if what he was about to say was somewhat far-fetched, "from his *wife*."

"Huh."

"Huh?" I said, not sure at all what his point was.

At the time, the only thing I knew about Yeats and wives was that he didn't get the one he wanted. In his poems, Yeats goes on and on and on about a woman who married someone else. I didn't know a single thing about the wife he actually got. The cloud hovered, ready to spill.

"Yeah," he said, sarcastically, "I guess she, like, pulled it out of a hat or something." He chuckled at this and rolled his eyes, assuming we'd all find this fact quite amusing.

And it happened just like that. I knew immediately that things had changed. The others turned their heads away from me and toward him, with serious concern. Nineteenth century novel guy actually shook his head helplessly, as if his friend had just walked out in front of a speeding car and it was too late to return to the safety of the sidewalk.

Feminist theory professor snapped her neck up as if being awakened from a deep sleep, which is actually quite possible, and the dark, dense storm cloud of doom that had threatened for forty five minutes to wash me out of the ranks of the educated altogether, left me alone. It shot straight across the small office, where it lodged itself just north of Renaissance poetry guy's ears.

Over my head was a cloudless, sunny sky, broad and wide as the heavens over the prairies. Everything seemed possible again. In that one instant I moved from subject of doom to observer of same, and that is no small move, let me tell you.

Renaissance guy stammered. He knew as well as the rest of us that he'd just let a really big one fly and that it would take a long time to move past this. "Well, I mean, I only mean, she was some kind of a psychic or at least she thought she was. It's not to say she wasn't intelligent or anything, only that she was kind of, well you know … "

"She pulled it out of a *what?*" feminist theory professor wanted to know. "Did you just say Yeats' wife pulled the notion of the gyre out of a hat?!"

I don't recall the conversation after that, except that it was tense and angry and I knew it had nothing whatsoever to do with me. The cloud remained over Renaissance guy's head and paid me no further attention.

Once feminist theory professor and the others were through with Renaissance guy, at least for the time being, they returned to face me, but by then the pressure was off. The hot seat was no longer mine. I was just another pleasant if nervous graduate student ready to answer some more questions, and so onward we went, happily together.

We talked about the romantic poets, and about labor writers from the 1930s, about Shakespeare and James Fennimore Cooper and even about Chaucer and the Wife of Bath, who was back in all of her saucy glory. The last half of the exam marched along quite pleasantly, so much so that I noted a slight hint of sorrow that the period was over, as delightful as it was to know some answers and chat with these fine people.

Don't get me wrong, I was also happy to leave. I left the room with a future in English and in teaching, and knew exactly how close I'd come to leaving with something very different. And I left more fond of Yeats' wife, a woman I'd known nothing about two hours previously, than any other character either within or married to the English and American literary canons.

Bulldogs

90% of Bulldogs in need of giving birth require, if they in-
tend to survive, a veterinarian willing and able to administer a C-
section. This is true for almost all Boston Terriers and Chihuahuas
too. And, according to what pops up on Google when I do a
completely non-methodical search, "not just *any* vet can do a successful C-section" (emphasis mine). The same website also offers
the following advice: "Boston Terriers are a man-made breed, and
cannot survive without a large amount of human intervention. If
this bothers you, then the Boston Terrier would not be a good
breed for you to try and raise/show." Yes, I suppose so. I also think
that if this bothers you then you and I would get along nicely.

When I see dogs whose genes have been severely messed with
by human beings, I am overcome with a desire to apologize to the
dogs as representatives of their species on behalf of my own. My
friends Lois and Connie have a couple of Shihtzus, and I actually
have apologized to both of them when their owners were not in
the room. I've gotten down on all fours myself to be nearer to the
beaver-sized animals, and looked right into their bulging, drippy
eyes to tell them how badly I feel about the whole mix-up.

Unlike much of what I find most unsettling in life, dog breeding is not a consequence of the Bush administration. It's not in
any way that I can find linked to the conditions of our consumer
economy, our swindling media system, or James Dobson and all

of his followers down in Colorado Springs. According to the D volume of my trusty 1973 World Book Encyclopedia, humans all over the planet have been breeding dogs for bizarre purposes for thousands of years.

Sure, dogs have been bred for hunting, herding, and other specific tasks all along, and that I can understand. In these cases, people only let reproduce those dogs that are the fleetest of foot, can fit into rats' holes, have the best sense of smell, and things like that. I want this to be the whole story, but that's just not the case.

The Chihuahua, for example, has been bred for "ceremonial purposes," and to exist for someone else's ceremonial purposes is no insignificant thing. Though there are competing theories about exactly how the breeding occurred and when, most breeding historians maintain that the Aztecs used the Chihuahua's ancestors as cremation sacrifices in order to atone for sins and guide dead people's spirits in the afterlife. The dogs were bred to be the most appropriate matches for their starring role in prevalent myth, a myth which held that a small red dog could help the soul cross the waters between this life and the next.

Now I like ceremonies as a general rule, as I have a flair for drama and wish we'd pause and commemorate the profound nature of events and emotions more often than we already do. But it would never occur to me to take an animal and decide what other animal it has sex with, and what animal its offspring will have sex with, and on and on for hundreds of years, so that I might have just the right sort of animal to sit on my lap during a particular ceremony.

Let's take the annual graduation ceremony at the local community college where I work, for example. I can try to imagine putting that kind of time and energy into a dog that might go best with my big black gown. A stark white would be the flashiest here, but maybe I should tone down the contrast; after all, graduation really is about the students. Maybe a regal, dark tone? A shiny coat would be nice. Should it have the temperament to sit still through the speeches and handing out of degrees, a thin-enough coat to allow it comfort in the overheated gym, and better yet, still be able to walk proudly next to me in the processional, touching all four paws to the gym floor in complete tandem with the Pomp and Circumstance being played by the local community band?

Overall, the whole thing just seems really unnecessary to me. Granted, there are ceremonial moments when I look at my own children and wish someone a few hundred years back had had the foresight to use just such a process so that our family wouldn't be so embarrassing in public, but these moments usually pass.

In England, the country that should win any award ever offered for having the weirdest fascination with dog-gene adjustment practices, Charles II surrounded himself with a type of little dog soon thereafter known as the Cavalier King Charles Spaniel. He then decreed that no such spaniel should be denied access to any public space, had his portrait painted with the dogs about a hundred times, and dictated that they should precede him down hallways and into grand rooms, including the rooms of parliament (which remain to this day, by the way, officially open to dogs of this kind).

After Charles suffered a stroke that required his soul to leave his body and go someplace else, perilously unaccompanied by a canine, the dog went out of fashion, and breeders left with the suddenly undesirable dogs decided to do what they do best. What the spaniel needed, they decided, was a flat face to replace his long nose and a domed head to replace his flat one. His flatness was discovered to exist in all the wrong places, a problem to which pubescent boys and girls the world over relate powerfully. So the breeders got to selecting for these qualities, and decades later the old long-nosed variety, the one that had been so very hip for a time, was nowhere to be found.

But despair not. As long as we had the paintings, it was only a matter of time before someone would seek to bring the dogs back.

And sure enough, in the last 80 years great care has been taken in monitoring the sexual activities of certain spaniels to make sure the old dog, the one seen in all of the king's paintings, is its own thriving, recognized, AKC breed. Whew. Now we're beyond breeding for ceremonial purposes and onto, what, breeding for art history's sake?

We also have a history of breeding dogs to entertain us, and this is where things get particularly disturbing. In some cases, dogs are bred for certain characteristics that make them most likely to engage in "silly antics in our sitting rooms." Imagine a young, hyperactive dog coming of age, asking his mother about his birth, only to be told he was bred specifically to perform silly antics. And yet this very scene has been played out thousands of times over the centuries, without a single support group or therapist or blog dedicated to helping the pups move on (though some few dogs are fortunate enough to snag prescriptions for Ritalin).

What I find most strange, however, is something that's not mentioned in any of the dog breed histories I can find. When a group of people needed a dog to rid houses of small rodents, the breed historians explain that a longer snout and a high state of alertness were desired and developed. But there is no explanation offered that might help us understand why other features of dogs were selected and encouraged. What is obvious to me, even if the historians and breeders don't like to say it out loud, is that we seem to breed certain dogs to look as much like people as possible, for the purpose of, well, I have no earthly idea.

For no reason I can find, other than to make some dogs look like us, we have so significantly shortened their snouts that there is no longer room inside of their mouths for their tongues. I guess it's not so easy to breed them for shorter tongues, as it is to simply breed away the mouth itself. So we make cooing noises and scratch the chins of these animals, ignoring the fact that several inches of dripping, dirty tongue hangs there, not knowing what to do with itself. Or their faces have been so altered that their eye sockets no longer fully enclose the eyeballs. It is not uncommon for a Pekinese's eyeballs to pop out of their sockets entirely. "What cute big eyes she has! Gracious, there they go again!" I am always uncomfortable around these creatures, because I can't decide whether they are caricatures of the dogs they once were, or of us. They make me feel like I'm at a creepy, themed costume party, only nobody told me what the theme was.

The Shihtzus that belong to my friends Lois and Connie have been given human names—well, soap opera human names anyway—Blair and Stephan, and are talked to, dressed up, and hauled around as if they were good looking and well behaved children, lack of evidence not withstanding. Lois and Connie, in fact, would take issue with the "as if" part of that last sentence, and would likely want to know just what, exactly, I was implying.

Of all the dogs out there, I don't understand why these poor schmucks with short snouts, harsh yips, and bulging eyes are the dogs people most enjoy pampering and treating like children, for if we see them as children, they are horrific images indeed. What would people think of a young kid whose face was permanently stained by the snot that its nose could not contain, or of a baby whose tongue was three times as long as its mouth cavity? I bet these kids would have a very hard time of it, and no less so with the ladies who cart their similarly featured dogs around with them to restaurants and stores, daring with a maternal, protective glare anyone who might suggest they are only "pets" and not allowed on the premises. Surely there are better looking, calmer, easier-on-the-ears dogs out there that we could pretend to rear as children. But we seem to have created these creatures specifically for this purpose, and I have to say I just don't get it.

Last week I brought my cat to the vet, and I met one of these women and Rebecca, her Chihuahua. As I sat in the waiting room next to the pet carrier that held my cat (though not recognized by any known feline organization I am fully confident that it is a pure, full-bred "cat"), a woman in her seventies entered while in the middle of a conversation with her dog. It was a full conversation that began before I saw them and continued after they left, except for the missing responses of the dog itself, responses that the woman appeared not to notice missing: "That's right Becky; we'll stop on the way home for some chicken. Would you like some chicken for lunch? I knew it. Do you want it shredded like we did last Tuesday for dinner? Cut into pieces? That'll be easy to do. Here's the doctor's office, Becky. Oh don't you go and fret. I won't let these people touch you more than necessary. You have nothing to worry about."

Personally, I thought the dog had a great deal to worry about, but, not knowing her well, I considered it not my part to intervene.

At every vet's office I've ever visited, the protocol is always the same: I check in at the front desk and then sit in a waiting room until I am called. Then a veterinarian's assistant comes out, takes the animal, and weighs it on a big electronic scale. The other day, there was nobody at the front desk when the woman walked in, though I don't think she would have stopped anyway. She took Rebecca out of her impressively manor-like pet carrier. Then she made her way behind the front desk and proceeded to weigh the dog herself:

"Stand on the little table for Mommy, Becky. That's it. I know; your mommy's right here. Just stand still so I can see your weight and I'll … OOoohh! You're getting to be fat aren't you Becky? Four point six pounds. You're getting chubby in your age. Well, it's that chicken, I know. Up you go. There there. Mommy's got you."

In the waiting room, the woman and I had a chance to chat. I kept hoping she would leave to use a restroom or something so that I could apologize to her dog, but that didn't happen. Instead, she greeted me and learned my name, and then looked at her dog and introduced me:

"Did you hear that? Her name is Saarraa, and she's here with her cat."

"Sara?" she continued, shifting her attention to me with a formal gravity that might have seemed appropriate if I were meeting the Governor, "this is Rebecca, my third Chihuahua. She is eleven years of age. I like to come in at this time of year and get everything taken care of before winter comes, because Rebecca *cannot* go outside when it's cold."

"Certainly not," I said, noting that the dog seemed to be in a constant state of shivering.

When an assistant eventually came to call the woman and her dog ("We can see Rebecca now") into a back room, the woman took quite a bit of her own sweet time putting Rebecca back in her pet carrier with such delicacy and care that you'd think the dog had seventeen bone fractures that had not yet been splinted. She then stood up somewhat more dramatically than anything the moment seemed to call for, with straight back and Rebecca's cage resting firmly against her thigh.

"We'll need her out of her cage to weigh her," said the vet assistant.

"Four point six. I've already done it."

"She'll still need to come out for her nail clipping," said the now tight-mouthed vet assistant.

"When she is at the doctor's, she prefers to be moved around in her carrier. Less drafty," said the woman.

"I'll. Carry. It. For. You. Then." said the vet assistant, reaching her hand toward Rebecca's carrier and forcing out one word of pleasantry at a time while struggling to keep her mouth from saying something it clearly wished to say.

But despite the vet assistant's attempts at diplomacy, at this very moment the woman actually smacked the assistant's hand away, sending a slight slapping noise through the room: "*I* will carry my Rebecca while we are here," she replied. And off they went, the vet assistant rolling her eyes as the woman preceded her out of the room, chest and chin thrust forward. In my experience, surprising things rarely happen at the vet's office. They charge a lot when the cats are fine and they charge a gross amount and then put them to sleep when they are not. So I felt fortunate to have been present to witness my very first, if very minor, assault on a veterinarian's assistant by a Chihuahua owner/Mommy.

While I worry about Rebecca and Blair and Stephan and other dogs out there that might have similar experiences, there is another breed among us that deserves much more than our especial sympathy, and this is the Bulldog. Exactly what it deserves I can't say, but I do know that in this case, an apology is woefully inadequate and any reparations would come far too late. When we compare the history of the Bulldog with that of Rebecca's unfortunate Aztec ancestors, I think most of us would agree that the Chihuahua got a luckier deal, even if being cremated because someone else has died and having the energy output needs of a herd of gazelle packed into a single, four-pound body may seem a bit harsh.

In the thirteenth century, the English developed a new national sport. Known for cricket and croquet, polo, rugby and the great pub sport, darts, the British have another old sporting tradition not often talked about anymore—Bullbaiting. There was some belief, though it's hard to know how widespread this was, that if a bull was made to be furious and terrified just before it was slaughtered, it would provide more tender meat than that of a bull who, say, had his life taken in the middle of a dream about daisies and long grass and pretty cows. It was also known, and this knowledge was both widespread and true, that the nose was one of the most sensitive areas on a bull's body. Therefore, people desirous of tender meat decided that the goal was to torture the nose of the bull before killing the entire body of the bull. This conclusion was logical for those wanting a good dinner, and problematic for English bulls, to be certain, but nobody could have anticipated its sporting potential.

Much to everyone's happy surprise, the people soon discovered that watching the eventually decided-upon method of said torture brought them great amounts of glee, and so the goal of tender meat at slaughter took a backseat to the entertainment value of the torture itself. The practice soon took on a celebratory purpose and was carried out on regular occasions with or without the eventual killing of the bull. And for the purpose of these celebrations, was bred the unlucky Bulldog, an ancestor of the well-known variety commonly seen today.

The bulldog wasn't chosen for this sport for its ability to sell tickets, or expensive, poor-quality beer and caramel corn; it wasn't chosen for its particular eye for decoration or to shepherd any stray toddlers back to the throng of the spectators. The early Bulldog was chosen for bull-baiting because it was known for its ferocity, tenacity, and, clearly, its lack of critical thinking skills. Once trained, it could be made to bite and hold onto just about anything, and, if it were particularly well-trained, would refuse to let go its grip even despite impending death.

The bull was paraded into a ring in front of the expectant audience, and then tied by a neck rope to a stake in the ground. At this point the bull was suspicious and on his way to getting downright pissed off. More astute than the bulldog, this animal had known our kind for long enough to know that the anxious and excited crowd didn't bode well for him.

Finally, the moment everyone had been waiting for arrived. Snack bags floated to the ground as the people swallowed their last bites and crying babies somehow sensed it was time to be quiet. A hush, as they say, befell the crowd. The bulldog was released and ordered to leap up and clamp onto the bull's nose with his great jaws. The bull would roar and buck and throw his body as violently as possible in his effort to rid himself of the terrifically painful creature biting his nose. The dog would hang there, taking in the face the full force of the snot and mucus rushing out of the nose in its mouth, its body being yanked up, down, sideways and every other way, refusing to let go. The people would hoot and holler and pee themselves in happiness. This is the element of human nature that liberals don't pay enough attention to, by the way. We're just never going to get it right if we don't acknowledge what Stephen King and the producers of reality TV already know: human beings like to watch suffering.

So, happy were the people. There was a problem, though, with the dogs. Many were killed in the sport; this was to be expected. Many others broke bones, often times most of them at once. And some dogs held on so tightly that they weren't thrown off until all of their teeth were ripped out. There was nothing to be done in these cases but go home to tell Irish jokes and enjoy a warm shepherd's pie. But the dog owners did wish, that in those cases when the dog was neither killed instantly nor broken to pieces nor left bleeding to death, that it could be saved for another rollicking day of bull-baiting. We're not an entirely wasteful species, after all. Just mostly. Unfortunately, the violent thrashing of the bull usually broke the spines of the dogs even before they were thrown, making them downright useless for future events.

What was needed? Some savvy dog breeding, of course. The people started breeding for a smaller but equally strong and tenacious dog, and they started breeding for a bigger head and chest and the smallest bottom half possible. This way, so the thinking went, most of the dog's weight would be located nearer to the center of the activity, and the lighter and smaller back end meant less weight yanking on the spine as it got tossed around. This resulted in fewer broken dog backs, and, therefore, more future happiness for the people. This also resulted in dogs that could not pass the enormous heads of their offspring through their tiny pelvic canals. If "not just any vet can do a successful C-section" now, in the infancy of the 21st century, how many could do it in England in the 14th century? It's not entirely clear how the species survived, though what is perfectly obvious is that its survival had nothing whatsoever do to with the species being asked whether or not it wished to survive.

Six hundred years after the sport first took hold, English bull baiting was made illegal in 1835. This makes sense, of course:

modern man got enlightened in the previous century, gaining confidence in human reason and moving on to make better decisions about everything from witches to chamber pots. So that should be the end of it, right? In the autumn of that year the dogs were taken into the backyards of the English, given dentist-approved chew toys that were specifically not bulls and a soft place to sleep, and then let free to run out in pastures and keep their teeth and vertebrae intact. That's how the story should go, but it doesn't. This is because the final and greatest indignity inflicted by humankind upon the Bulldog, no kidding, was yet to be introduced.

Once bull baiting was no longer acceptable in the eyes of the law, the English found themselves with a lot of dogs without a purpose. It must have been like buying thirty-seven cases of sparklers only to come home and read in the papers that the Fourth of July has been voided out, erased from the nation's memory and calendars everywhere. Bulldogs held no promise as lapdogs and were too ferocious to be much fun at suddenly-hip, non-violent parties. The people remained fond of the dogs however, having enjoyed them for such a long time, and were not ready to let them wander off to have a breather in the damp woods before dying in puppybirth. Instead, ("Say Nigel, I have a great idea ... ") they decided some more—you guessed it—breeding was in order. They began to select against ferocity and to exaggerate the big head, short snout, and tiny pelvis features of the dog even further. This way they could have their beloved bulldogs around to remind them of the good old days, looking more ferocious than ever, without fearing they'd lose a hand or a toddler's left leg at any given moment. The bulldog is not the only species known for its tenacity. Can't we ever learn to just give it a rest?

So what we're left with, after all that, is a Bulldog who for 600 years was used as a torture-for-human-kicks organism, but which then had its very ability to feel the ferocity it had been known for all along sucked right out of its DNA. Surely there never was an animal that deserved to feel more angry than this one, but even that most appropriate emotional response was denied it.

Now the breed is known for its strange physical features and its amiable personality, neither having been the choice of the Bulldogs, or, need I mention, the forces of evolution. I don't know what the bulldog's next genetically-controlled developments might entail, but I'm not hopeful it will be pretty. I'll keep apologizing when I get the chance, but I'll understand when my gesture is met with less than full gratitude and forgiveness. If the dog is indifferent or her body posture too hard to read, I'll let it go at that. The truth is, at this point, there's really very little a person can say to the Bulldog without raising a whole host of ugly questions about the human being. Perhaps it really is best to dress it up in children's clothes and pretend that we've meant well all along.

Liquid Latex: Blue

Humor is heroic, if you can pull it off. It's heroic like the Royal Canadian Mounted Police are heroic when they untie damsels from the railroad tracks just as speeding locomotives approach. It's heroic because it saves people against really bad odds. But those odds are bad for a reason. Most of the time the train hits the damsel. Or it hits the Mountie. Or it derails because the Mountie left his awkward hat on the tracks after discovering that the report of a damsel tied to the tracks was a ruse, of course, because how trite, and the accident leaves twelve dead, thirty wounded, and an environmental disaster caused by the leakage of a toxic chemical. It's risky business, humor is.

So you'll understand why I thought this would be funny, I have to tell you about my family. We have a boy, two and a half, and another boy, one and a half, and so daily life works because of routine. The routine helps the boys—they don't know how to wind down toward bedtime unless we go through our regular steps of bath, teeth brushing, pajamas, milk, books, lights out, songs on laps, songs in bed. But most of the daytime routine is in place just for our sanity, I think. I have to know that if I make it to seven, bath time, then I will be ok. And I have to know that nap time is coming right after lunch, and that I can count on one of the kids to eat well at either lunch or dinner, but not both, and that neither of them will eat much for breakfast despite sometimes very high levels of anticipation about the pancakes or eggs or cereal, because if I didn't know this, I'd go crazy every time they neglected the food I'd prepared so carefully. And I have to know that at five minutes after eight, I can run around the block, or drink a beer and sit and say nothing, or grade papers, or talk to my partner for the hour or two we have before we both collapse, stunned.

Anyway, like I said, I thought it would be funny. We'd been looking for months for a color for our very drab old kitchen, wanting badly to make it at least appear to be a cleaner space, but failing quite definitively with our color choices. We spent $100 on one color we believed in, only to get it on the wall and realize it would do nothing to take away the drab, but instead accentuated it, something I didn't know possible with drab.

But my partner and I have little time to sit down in the same room and have a conversation, because, as I said, of two very short people who live with us and have a large number of needs from moment to moment. So except for the last hour of the day—and then only if one of us is not rushing to accomplish a lot or rushing to squeeze in time to accomplish nothing at all—except for that rare moment, we do most of our talking over email from work.

But conversations about colors for the kitchen are hard to have on email, so two months ago I found myself looking online, hoping to find some color samples that we could discuss digitally, as it were. I went to Google and gave it my best shot with the two minutes I had available, and of course, while I didn't find any color palates, I did find links to other bizarrely-related word phrases. One that engaged me and ultimately led me down the path I now disclose, not without shame, was about colored body paints. The link took me to an online costume shop, which was selling big jars of body paints for only eight bucks a pop. All of a sudden I was overcome with visions of those blue guys in Chicago—I don't know what they do, but have seen their images on postcards and in the arts and entertainment section of our newspaper—and I immediately ordered a jar of blue. Of course I did. I am not made up of the stuff it would take to say no to such an offer. Eight bucks to be a blue person for an hour? Of course. Please send it, post haste.

It arrived in a box, about ten inches square, and sat for a week or two on our dining room table. After the boys were told seventeen times they could not open it, they lost interest and ignored it. My partner asked every few days what was in it, and seemed slightly disconcerted about the return address. But I didn't fess up, of course, because I had this plan see, a plan to break into our routine with the funniest damn thing the three of them had seen in a long time, giving us all a break from the dinner at six, bath at seven, books at seven-thirty, bed at eight routine that really I have to say, despite its benefits, can get a little dry. I thought I'd wait until there was a good time, run into the bathroom and become blue person, and jump out much to everyone's delight. I hadn't figured out whether I should wear clothes or not—do the blue guys? In fact I hadn't figured on much, not having read the instructions or warnings on the jar, not having thought about what I was doing at all, except that I was certain it was going to be funny.

So a day arrived that found us sitting in the back yard at our picnic table, finishing a dinner. We eat out there most every day of the summer, partly because we like to be outside and a lot because the hose and squirrels and the ten-dollar plastic swimming pool only yards away cut down on our cleaning time by about 70%. The kids were still at the table and not upset about it or refusing to eat or throwing things, and my partner was calmly talking with them. The moment's arrived, I thought to myself. Hurrah! I announced I'd be right back with a surprise for them all, and, quite pleased with myself, ran inside, grabbed the box off the table, and headed into the bathroom to strip off my clothes. My partner was still outside, and as I left the yard I heard her asking the boys what they thought I'd do: come out with a lion mask on? They roared happily. Come out as a snake? They hissed and laughed. But eventually, likely about thirty seconds later, their calm was disturbed by their natural state and they needed to move onto other things.

In the bathroom I ripped open the box and opened the jar, dug my hand in up to my wrist, and started hastily slopping the goo all over my feet and legs. The fumes affected me suddenly and were, well, toxic; they had overwhelmed me by the time the blue had covered only my feet and ankles, so I had to run to the window, which was cracked open two inches, to breathe. I was undaunted though, and I gulped in some air and went back to what I was doing—slapping this stuff all over my body, not caring that it also flew in all directions, splattering itself on the bathtub, on the toilet, on the bathmat, and the floor. I spared my midsection, deciding that I'd put shorts and a t-shirt back on, a decision I now realize was made by a voice of sanity I am happy to carry around in my subconsciousness. I'd be happier still if I carried it around at a level more accessible in my daily life, but I've learned to be grateful it's in there at all.

Anyway, blue I became, and fast, but I was also experiencing a tightening of my skin that was becoming most uncomfortable. And I was beginning to notice that if I touched a blue part of my body to another blue part, the two parts would stick together, painfully. But still I was driven by my belief that this would be funny, and all of this was therefore worth it, and besides, how does one turn back at this point? I was having a harder and harder time breathing, and my eyes were watering heavily. By the time my arms and neck were becoming blue, I was only breathing by the window and holding my breath during the intervals. I slapped the stuff up and around the back of my neck, and onto my face.

My plan, of course, was to be totally covered. I had not yet acknowledged my unconscious decision to spare my midsection and now was confronted with another problem. The closer it got to my eyes, the more violent the fumes—and really breathing was

very difficult and becoming painful—so I couldn't get it quite
right up around the eyes, and instead left an inch or so of plain
skin exposed around each one. But the eyebrows got coated nicely;
they are thick and so sucked in quite a bit of this stuff, and the
forehead too. I coated my ears, of course, but then that same voice
that spared my midsection told me to also forego the most of my
hair. Again, I didn't choose to investigate this decision. It would
have made me acknowledge that I looked ridiculous, that my fingers were stuck together and part of my arm stuck to part of my
side where blue had gotten rubbed accidentally, that I didn't look
anything at all like the blue guys from Chicago but more like,
well, a complete and utter freak, one who had experienced an
inexplicable accident involving waste material.

The little bits of blue that had found their way into my hair
made my hair bunch and stick up in hard clumps. My eyes stuck
out grotesquely, surrounded by pale skin, which was itself surrounded by hastily and sloppily applied strange blue goop. The
rest of my body was equally a mess. The paint was unevenly applied, so in places my flesh showed through, and in others it didn't.
And I had to get out of the room, as I was unable to hold my
breath any more long enough for me to do anything and my lungs
ached with increasing ferocity. So that had to be it. As best I could,
I pulled on my shorts and t-shirt and opened the door.

I appreciated very much the burst of fresh air that I encoun-
tered in the hallway, but yelped at the pain caused by my shorts
and shirt sticking to the paint, which was in turn stuck to my
body hair, meaning that every tug of either garment led directly
to the ripping out of said body hair. Anyway my eyes continued
to water, but now from the pain of having hairs ripped out or
pulled rather than fumes.

Still, I was driven, though by now my motivation was shifting. Foremost in my mind remained my belief that I was about to
make my family laugh hysterically, but my need for assistance and
relief was beginning to take a firmer hold in the arena of my clouded

consciousness. As I walked through the dining room and kitchen, looking to burst outside where I hoped naively they were still sitting at the table, I started to cry a little bit, because the pain was really quite unbearable, and my shorts and shirt, while officially on, were stuck sort of half way on, because I couldn't get them any further on and I couldn't get them off, being attached to my skin and body hair as firmly as they were. The shirt ended up sort of bunched around my chest and upper arms, mostly but not completely covering my breasts and pulling one arm out and back. So by the time I reached the back door, I was only a tiny bit still hoping it would still be funny, and mostly desperate to find my partner so she could help me, as I thought I couldn't stand it any longer. She was just then in the process of herding the two boys into the house, after some incident or another had caused one of them much stress, and she looked up to me, as did they, wondering where I'd been and why I was in their way, the two little ones having forgotten entirely about the whole, "Mama Sara's going to come out with a surprise" business.

My announcement, once envisioned as a victorious "I'm blue!" came out more like a meek question than anything else. "I'm blue?" I murmured, with arms outstretched as much as I was able, which was different on each side, owing to the tug of the t-shirt and the paint gluing me together in so many ways, so that I looked a crooked cross, not just a freak now—the best freaks have an elegance about them that buttresses their defiance of normalcy—but a graceless and broken one. I made my announcement partly as if with exclamation mark, and partly with a notable whimper, because every movement was now excruciating. The boys stared—at my legs, at my middle with my clothes all askew and only partly where they were supposed to be. They stared at my exposed belly, with splotches of bright red skin where the blue had been ripped away and splotches of the blue and the rest just my pale regular stomach. If you've ever had the misfortune to appear on one of our popular daytime television talk shows, the ones that serve the

cultural function once filled by freak shows, if you've ever inten-
tionally freakified yourself or your intimate relationships for commercial display on television, and while doing so have had the
guts and the imagination to consider how your national audience
was looking at you, then you already know the look on the faces
of my two sons out there on the back porch. It's not an experience
I would particularly recommend.

I didn't look at my partner's face, I suppose because I was by
then so far involved in the inevitable experience of shame to do
so, but simply declared I was in great pain and would take a bath
immediately. I turned to leave them as quickly as I'd met them
just ten seconds before, and as I did so I heard a slow, oncoming
whimper from one of the boys, a sound that was amplified and in
stereo by the time I reached the bathroom, and which became
two full-fledged cries of horror by the time I'd ripped off my clothes
and all the hairs they were stuck to and stepped into the tub. I
don't know what noises I was making at the time, and am glad I
have protected myself from that particular detail of memory, as I
don't guess they were any more eloquent than my appearance.

I had happened to notice when first opening the jar of paint
the phrase "wash with soap and water," and so I had every reason
to believe the bath would offer fast relief, and figured the absur-
dity of the evening, embarrassing as it has been, was at least almost over. I'd wash it off, my partner would calm the boys down,
I'd come out my regular old self, and they'd be ok. We'd forget this
incident as quickly as possible, using my bravado about the stunt
and apparent inability to remember any pain (Nah, it didn't hurt
much), and by reading a lot of books repetitively and singing our
usual songs with especial gusto.

But things didn't turn out the way I hoped at that dark moment either, for the boys' cries only increased in intensity as my
partner tried to buy their complacency with ice cream, and then,
just as I buckled my knees into a squat so that I might sit in the
bathtub, my legs stuck together, the hairs of the backs of my thighs

suddenly cemented to the hairs on the backs of my calves. I couldn't stand or sit, but just teetered there on my toes in a deep and painful squat. It was also becoming clear to me that the goo was by no means whatsoever, under any circumstances, water-soluble.

So there was one son, hollering in a high chair with a bowl of ice cream he had no interest in so that he at least couldn't come into the bathroom and witness an even worse version of the horror that had sent him into hysterics in the first place; there was the older son, standing in the door of the bathroom gawking—the kid couldn't even close his mouth—and whimpering and crying in a way that required no facial movement. You'd have thought his cry came from another child, had there been that possibility, because his face didn't so much as twitch. There was my partner—to whom I've re-committed the rest of my life precisely because by this point in the evening she had not uttered one single word of judgment—trying to soothe the younger son stuck in his high chair and to coax the older son from the doorframe, that he might rest his eyes on something far less terrifically strange and calm down.

And there was me, crying out for help in my own desperate effort to unglue my legs, first and foremost. As I pulled them apart, feeling hairs go on both sides, a sort of web appeared. It was like the stuff in between the fingers and toes of Aquaman, only it kept me from standing or sitting and did not enable me to swim or save the world. Scissors, we thought, and off she ran to collect them. When she returned, both boys still horrified and crying, my remaining body hairs still being pulled mercilessly, she lunged in to try to cut the web in hopes of disconnecting my thighs from my calves. As she did this I waived my freest arm around maniacally, trying to peel patches off where I could, which was almost nowhere. In the confusion, the scissors took off the corner of the tip of one of my fingers. We noted this briefly with a gasp from me and a good thirty-second knee slapping stint of laughter from my partner, and then pressed on. The pain of body hair being pulled far outweighed the new injury, so I held that hand up to keep it out of the way and returned to my frantic grasping and peeling with the other arm, the one still partially attached to my side, while she returned to her effort to disconnect my legs.

When the blood came trickling down my finger and arm, it added a startling new color to the scene. The bright red stood out in the sea of blues and whites of the bathroom like a brightly colored car in an otherwise black and white advertisement, enhancing my sense that I was in a different space, a liminal, digitally enhanced space maybe, but not the reality of my life.

Eventually my oldest son left the room of his own accord to go and have a good long cry elsewhere, and my partner left me alone to pick at my skin and hair. Slowly I did manage to uncover my regular body. My partner eventually discovered a chemical in the bathroom closet that saved me from having to shave my eyebrows, and by the end of the evening I was ok. I was pink and mostly free of body hair and still in some places sticky, but we knew I'd live. We read our usual books and sang our usual songs, and the kids took a bath at seven and went to bed at eight. They didn't bring it up again.

Every now and then my partner will ask the kids, "do you remember when Mama Sara got blue?" as if probing for any pent up trauma that they might need to talk about. Both respond only with blank looks, and they change the subject as fast as they can, a gesture I appreciate fully. It's a risky business, this heroism duty, and a person appreciates all the forgiveness she can get.